Self-Presentation and Representative Politics

Self-Presentation and Representative Politics

Essays in Context, 1960–2020

Derek Robbins

ANTHEM PRESS

Anthem Press
An imprint of Wimbledon Publishing Company
www.anthempress.com

This edition first published in UK and USA 2025
by ANTHEM PRESS
75–76 Blackfriars Road, London SE1 8HA, UK
or PO Box 9779, London SW19 7ZG, UK
and
244 Madison Ave #116, New York, NY 10016, USA

First published in the UK and USA by Anthem Press in 2022

British Library Cataloguing-in-Publication Data
A catalogue record for this book is available from the British Library.

Library of Congress Control Number: 2024944085

ISBN-13: 978-1-83999-370-1 (Pbk)
ISBN-10: 1-83999-370-7 (Pbk)

Cover image: Details from Jacques-Louis David:
Le Sacre de Napoléon [The coronation of Napoleon], 1807.

This title is also available as an e-book.

CONTENTS

SOURCES

Chapter 1B was submitted in application for a Trevelyan Scholarship in 1962 – unpublished.

Chapter 2B was chapter 2, Part II, of my PhD thesis entitled 'Literature and Natural Philosophy, 1770–1800. The Relation between Scientific Systems and Literary Fictions with Special Reference to Joseph Priestley and Samuel Traylor Coleridge,' 1972 – unpublished (Cambridge University Library, ms. reading room. PhD. 8214 https://doi.org/10.17863/CAM.17310).

Chapter 3B was a paper given in November 1993 to the New Ethnicities Unit, University of East London, which was subsequently published internally as a working paper of the unit in 1995. It was reproduced, in March 1998 as 'Reflections on Citizenship and Nationhood. From Brubaker's Account on France and Germany,' *Franco-British Studies: Journal of the British Institute in Paris*, no. 23, Spring 1997, pp. 89–107, and again as Part II, chapter 19 of my *On Bourdieu, Education and Society*, 2006, 429–48.

Chapter 4B was a paper presented at a conference on 'Political Representation' organised by the Department of Social Politics, Languages and Linguistics at Duncan House, UEL (June 1999) – unpublished.

Chapter 5B was a keynote address to an international conference on Durkheim ('In search of solidarity: 150 years after the birth of Emile Durkheim') held in Oxford, 10–12 October 2008: This paper was subsequently published as 'From Solidarity to Social Inclusion: The Political Transformations of Durkheimianism'. *Durkheimian Studies*, 2011, 17, no. 1, pp. 80–102.

Chapter 6B was a keynote address at the BSA Bourdieu Study Group's 2nd Biennial International Conference: *Reproduction and Resistance*, at the University of Lancaster (July 2018) – unpublished.

NOTES ON TEXT

Some of the six texts have been reduced in length. Substantial omissions are indicated by the insertion of […] in the text. I have removed the statistical appendices from Chapter 1B. Otherwise the texts have been reproduced as first produced.

The references for texts 1B, 2B, 3B, and 4B are contained in those texts, in footnotes, as originally produced. Texts 5B and 6B used the Harvard referencing system. Therefore the details of the references in those two texts and for the Introduction, the background pieces, and the Postscript are assembled in the References section at the end of the book.

Lockdown has delayed the establishment of an archive at the University of East London which is intended to hold my papers and publications as well as documentation relevant to the history of the institution. This work is in progress. I mark with an asterisk those of my unpublished papers which should be found in this archive.

In referring to texts, 1960 [1920] indicates that a quotation is taken from a 1960 edition of a text first published in 1920. In this instance, I do not normally provide the details of the original publication.

Similarly, 1960; 1980 indicates that a quotation is taken from a text published in French in 1960 and in English translation in 1980. Both texts are normally referenced separately in the References. Sometimes I provide page references for quotations for both language versions.

PREFACE

I am delighted that Anthem Press has decided to release this book as a paperback. The text is unchanged from the hardback edition except for this brief note.

Since the book was completed and published in 2021/22, there have been four new UK prime ministers and a degree of political mayhem. It has become a common theme in political commentary in the UK during this period to suggest that the public has lost its trust in its politicians. One theme of this book is that the problem is not just that of the character and behaviour of individual politicians as people but, more, that elements of the representative system are not functioning in the interest of the people. It is indicative of the systemic malaise that common discourse seems to regard populism – whether of the 'left' or of the 'right' – as the enemy of democracy when democratic representation should be the procedure in place to bring the needs and aspirations of people into the decision-making of government. One chapter of the book (6B) highlights the view of Pierre Bourdieu that the 'political field' as a system is constantly susceptible to constitution and re-constitution by the people, for the people. The political system can respond historically to changing social needs. It is not the absolute property of professional 'parliamentarians' but a set of procedures enabling members of parliament to reflect the views of their constituents and to enact measures that take account of these views. Another chapter (4B) considers an analysis of Burke's speech on political representation given to the electors of Bristol in 1774 made by Ernest Barker in 1930 shortly after the passing of the Equal Franchise Act of 1928 which had extended the proportion of the adult population entitled to vote to 90 per cent as opposed to only 27 per cent at the beginning of the century.

Social changes necessitate political reform. In the General Election of 4 July 2024, 335 new members of parliament were elected. The re-issue of this book corresponds with this opportunity to re-set the relationship between political representatives and the people they represent.

Derek Robbins
August 2024

ACKNOWLEDGEMENTS

The normal acknowledgement of help and support in writing a book is completely inadequate for this text. From the time when we met and married in the late 1960s, the thoughts and actions of my wife, Diana, and I have been completely interconnected. The drift of the book, as indicated in the introduction, is to argue against the current tendency to conceive of self-definition and self-presentation predominantly in terms of interpersonal relations rather than by reference to objective cultures. This does not imply a rejection of the interpersonal. To convey the significant influences of family and social relations would involve a totally different kind of narrative which I am not attempting here. The three kinds of 'cultural capital', differentiated by Bourdieu, which I discuss in the Postscript, apply in a similar way in respect of 'social capital'. I want to acknowledge clearly that Diana's contribution has not just been supportive but fundamentally constitutive.

INTRODUCTION

This book is not *about* 'self-presentation'. It is rather more *about* 'representa-tive politics', but my discussion of this subject is not abstract. It is systemat-ically linked to an account of the process of my attitude formation through time (my developing self-constitution and self-presentation). The emergent attitude towards representative politics which the book displays is overtly rela-tive to my personal social and intellectual trajectory. This historical account culminates in the argument that political processes should be re-defined by re-assigning primacy to social encounters. This concluding argument tries to reverse the current trend in which self-reliant social discourse is proscribed politically. The form adopted in the book is a device to seek to enact what it finally argues. The historical account of my intellectual progression is offered as a model for reflexive socio-analytic exchanges within society, designed simultaneously to encourage mutual understanding between socially con-stituted individuals and to discourage acquiescence in the domination of professionalised politics.

The book assembles six papers which I have written during the course of my career, from 1962 until the present, all of which impinge on politics. Each is prefaced by a short introduction which gives an account of the circumstances of its production and offers some retrospective discussion of content and con-text. The individual chapters written at different times with varying emphases are threaded together through a developing analytical framework consol-idated by my encounter with Bourdieu. A line of development is evident from the chapter taken from my PhD with its philosophical concerns, closer to a history of ideas approach (Chapter 2B), in part reprised two decades later in a more structured sociological analysis of citizenship and nation-hood in a Bourdieusian manner (which is only sketched out in Chapter 3B). In Chapter 4B, I am engaged in an argument, via Burke and Barker, about electoral politics that attempts to expose the static symbolic representations of MPs to a sociology of the origins and life trajectories of competing politicians. A brief return to the details of a local political sub-field in the final chapter (6B) brings the reader full circle, now more fully buttressed by Bourdieusian phenomenology. A postscript reflects on the tripartite divisions of cultural capital over the course of an academic career and its determinants.

Consistent with my adherence to the thinking of Pierre Bourdieu whom I first met in 1986 and with whose work my own has been closely associated since that date, my procedure in this book is modelled on two of his late publications: *Le bal des célibataires*, 2002b, translated as *The Bachelors Ball*, 2008 (Bourdieu, 2002b, 2008) and *Esquisse pour une auto-analyse*, 2004, translated as *Sketch for a Self-Analysis*, 2007 (Bourdieu, 2004, 2007). In the first, Bourdieu assembled three long articles which he had written about his native Béarn at intervals of about a decade, introduced by a short, retrospective preface written in July 2001. There was an affinity between his reflection here on the correlation between the social changes in the Béarn and his periodic conceptualisations of them and his final text in which he extended this reflection so as to consider his whole life 'auto-analytically' rather than autobiographically, that is to say, to analyse objectively, rather than subjectively, the social conditions of his social and intellectual trajectory. Famously, Bourdieu began his *Sketch for a Self-Analysis* with the statement that 'I do not intend to indulge in the genre of autobiography' (Bourdieu, 2007, 1). He wanted to show how he had been constituted by the 'fields' which impinged upon his trajectory rather than as a result of individual volition. That is why he commences his account with a commentary on the intellectual field which he entered in the 1950s rather than with a description of his family background. In this way, he wanted his final reminiscences to endorse the theory about the relationship between 'habitus' and 'field' which he had developed during his career. While I am sympathetic to this approach, I have no comparable need to adopt exactly the same method in representing my self-development. Rather, my autobiographical commentaries are designed to explore the problem of 'relevance' – what Bourdieu liked to characterise as the phenomenon of 'elective affinity' – to ask what it was in my trajectory which caused me, in my 40s, to find it useful to adopt the explanatory framework which Bourdieu had adopted in his. As such, this text is an exercise in demonstrating the pragmatic value of Bourdieu's conceptual framework rather than one of asserting its universal validity. This is an extended personal elaboration of the contention objectively offered in my *The Bourdieu Paradigm* (Robbins, 2019).

I present six texts in relation to my career and social trajectory. Following Bourdieu's adherence to Cassirer's view that 'the real is relational', this means that they are to be assessed and understood relationally rather than absolutely. I am not merely seeking to imitate Bourdieu's *method* of presentation in *The Batchelors' Ball*. Rather this book is an extension and application of Bourdieu's total thinking.

With specific reference to politics, I am trying to pursue further the approach which I have taken to Bourdieu's work since his death. In *On Bourdieu, Education and Society*, (Robbins, 2006), I wrote a long introduction which situated 25 reproduced articles in relation to my career development to that date. This was my first attempt, by reference to my personal case, to analyse the way in which I, as an English academic, had gradually, understood, interpreted, communicated within the English intellectual field texts which Bourdieu had produced within the French intellectual field in response to French social conditions. I became essentially interested in the transcultural transfer of ideas and in the problem of 'relevance' – how one nation state or culture receives the products of another. I tried to analyse the same problem objectively in *French Post War Social Theory: International Knowledge Transfer* (Robbins, 2011) which examined the production and reception of the work of Althusser, Aron, Foucault, Lyotard and Bourdieu. My *Cultural Relativism and International Politics* (Robbins, 2014) moved consideration of Bourdieu's cultural relationalism into contact with the analysis of international politics, highlighting the implications of the differences between Aron and Bourdieu. In *The Anthem Companion to Bourdieu* (Robbins, 2016) I deliberately invited contributors from different cultures to reflect on the nature of the reception of Bourdieu's work in their own countries, with a view, again, to highlighting whether the international exchange of ideas should occur within a fabricated international 'field' or should be the consequence of encounter between differences, whether, in other words, international politics should occur within a common framework imposed by dominant powers or should accommodate subordinate world views. My most recent book on Bourdieu – *The Bourdieu Paradigm. The Origins and Evolution of an Intellectual Social Project* (Robbins, 2019) – suggests that Bourdieu's sociology is best understood as an actualisation of Merleau-Ponty's phenomenological philosophy. This means that I think Bourdieu saw social 'reality' as the construct of plural social agents competing for dominance and that, increasingly, he sought to articulate the view that the future welfare of mankind depends on the capacity equitably to recognise the validity of plural positions. I have recently completed a translation of G. Gadoffre et al.'s *Vers le style du XXe siècle* (1945) and have written a commentary which contextualises its production (Robbins, 2021). The French text was the collaborative product of nine authors who held ideologically different positions but who could agree on a manifesto advocating a changed attitude towards human living. Emanating from the conflict of the Second World War, it was an attempt to suggest a blueprint for social reconstruction. My interest is not exclusively in the *content* of their recommendations. My commentary analyses how the content relates to the social backgrounds and previous careers of the authors and how they

4 SELF-PRESENTATION AND REPRESENTATIVE POLITICS

succeeded in their attempts during the rest of their lives to implement their manifesto.

Similarly, I am currently translating Tomoo Otaka's *Grundlegung der Lehre vom sozialen Verband* (*Outline of a Theory of Social Association*) (Otaka, 2022 (forthcoming)). Otaka was born and educated in Korea when it was under Imperial Japanese rule. He spent three years in Austria/Germany between 1929 and 1932, just before the rise of Hitler and, on returning to the East, became professor of law in Tokyo. Again, I am not primarily concerned with the pros and cons of the *content* of the book. I am interested in the phenomenon of the social conditions of production of the text, situated at the crossroads of Western European/Asian relations.

I should clarify a little further in relation to Bourdieu's project. It is well known that Bourdieu's fundamental conceptual framework was that all individuals inherit dispositions to act as a consequence of their family upbringing (*habitus*). This was not a deterministic position. It was a kind of 'soft determinism'. We all deploy our inherited dispositions in relation to or in response to ideas and values which are current in our society. These current values are not absolute. They happen to be the dominant values of the day. Quite possibly our inherited dispositions are marginal or excluded. Wherever we are located by birth and upbringing on a continuum from dominant to dominated within our society, we all have to decide strategically how far to subscribe to these dominant values or how far to articulate our inherited dispositions with a view to trying to make these become the dominant values in our society. Bourdieu admired those 'revolutionaries' who, in their fields, deployed the accredited 'cultural capital' which they acquired in dominant institutions as a Trojan horse to subvert that domination and elevate their indigenous values. He argued, for instance, that it was Édouard Manet's initiation into dominant artistic taste in his training at the École des Beaux Arts that enabled him to generate his particular form of impressionism, or that it was the training that André Courrèges received in the haute couture house of Balenciaga which enabled him to launch his subversive fashion innovations in the 1960s. In neither case was revolution independent of precedent.

The title of this book recalls two influential books. The first half connotes Erving Goffman's *The Presentation of Self in Everyday Life*, first published in 1959 (Goffman, 1969), and, less directly, the second half reflects much of the discussion in Jürgen Habermas's *Strukturwandel der Öffentlichkeit*, first published in 1962 and translated into English in 1989 as *The Structural Transformation of the Public Sphere* (Habermas, 1989 [1962]). It is important to define my bearings in relation to both.

Goffman wrote in his preface to *The Presentation of Self in Everyday Life* that his book would 'consider the way in which the individual in ordinary work situations presents himself and his activity to others, the ways in which he guides and controls the impression they form of him, and the kinds of things he may and may not do while sustaining his performance before him' (Goffman, 1969, 9). In a later book, *Relations in Public* (Goffman, 1971), Goffman published a short 'Author's Note' in which he indicated that the new book continued 'the consideration of face-to-face interaction developed in three previous books, *Encounters, Behaviour in Public Places* and *Interaction Ritual.*' (Goffman, 1971, 11). Although Goffman's first book, *Asylums*, analysed the experience of individuals in a constrained situation, his orientation was to focus on individuals more than on the constitutive effect of their institutional context: 'My immediate object in doing field work at St. Elizabeth's was to try to learn about the social world of the hospital inmate, as this world is subjectively experienced by him' (Goffman, 1961, 7). Goffman's key conception in *The Presentation of Self in Everyday Life* is that the behaviour of individuals is performative, both proactive presentation of self and reactive self-constitution as a consequence of the gauging of actual or predicted responses. The nature of the individual acting self is neglected or assumed. Goffman's actors improvise. They do not re-present a pre-existent script. Goffman transposed to the social sphere J. L. Austin's performative philosophy of language.

The socio-analytic encounter recommended by Bourdieu is very different from Goffman's face-to-face interaction. Bourdieu wrote a short obituary of Goffman in 1982, entitled 'Goffman, le découvreur de l'infiniment petit' (the discoverer of the infinitely small) (Bourdieu, 1982a) which acknowledged the richness of Goffman's analyses while arguing that they failed to attend to the large-scale structural contexts within which the analysed encounters occurred. For Bourdieu, Goffman's face-to-face encounters were conceived to be too exclusively inter-subjective without sufficient reference either to the objective determinants of encountering selves or to the influence of the specific objectivities of the situations framing those encounters. Bourdieu's objection to Goffman's work was similar to his disapproval of the influence in the early 1960s of what he took to be the de-socialised semiology of Roland Barthes. In his introduction in 1971 to the collection of essays which first brought the work of Bourdieu to the attention of the English-speaking world, Michael F. D. Young noticed what it was that clearly distinguished Bourdieu's work from that of contemporary ethnomethodologists. The collection contained an essay by Nell Keddie in which she showed 'how teachers construct their knowledge about pupils and how this relates not only to what knowledge they make available to pupils, but also to the way they scan pupil classroom activity for appropriate and expected meanings' (Young, 1971, 10). Keddie analysed the face-to-face encounters within the classroom. By contrast, Young observed that the analyses in the two essays by Bourdieu in the collection were 'essentially [...] structural' (Young, 1971, 12). This meant that Bourdieu focused on 'the interrelations of the pedagogic and curricular practices of the French school system and how they maintain the styles of thought characteristic of French academic culture' (Young, 1971, 12). In other words, for Bourdieu, interaction within the classroom was not just interpersonal but also involved the transmission of content whose objective existence had some prior status. The essence of Bourdieu's position was not yet apparent in English translation, but his *La reproduction* (Bourdieu and Passeron, 1970) argued that this content, although historically and culturally contingent, was, nevertheless, a real presence within pedagogical communication.

This holds true, for Bourdieu, of all social interaction. This distinction between the view of interaction as interpersonally and existentially self-sufficient, and the view that it always occurs in the context of socially constructed, but existent, objectivities, is fundamental. I recently explored the origins of Bourdieu's thought in this respect in the similar distinction between the work of Alfred Schutz and that of Aron Gurwitsch and, by extension, between the work of Sartre and Merleau-Ponty. The distinction is clear, for instance, in Merleau-Ponty's critique of the position adopted by Sartre in his preface to a new edition of Paul Nizan's *Aden Arabie*. Sartre regretted that he had not been as politically active in his youth as Nizan had been. Commenting on the preface, Merleau-Ponty suggested that 'there are two ways of being young' (Merleau-Ponty, 1960, 45; 1964, 25). Some 'are fascinated by their childhood' while others 'believe that they have no past and are equally near to all possibilities'. 'Sartre was one of the second type', whereas, by implication, Merleau-Ponty was of the first.[1] This is not just a matter of a difference of attitude towards one's childhood. What is at issue is a difference between thinking that an unconstrained, free self has the capacity to construct its essence – 'existence comes before essence' – (Sartre), and thinking that this 'self' has been formed and is constantly re-formed in a dialectical relationship with objective or pre-existing constraints (Merleau-Ponty). As Merleau-Ponty stated his position towards the end of *Phénoménologie de la perception*: 'To be born is both to be born of the world and to be born into the world. The world is already constituted, but also never completely constituted; in the first case we are acted upon, in the second we are open to an infinite number of possibilities' (Merleau-Ponty, 1945, 517; 1962, 453).

The work of Erving Goffman was informed by the work of Alfred Schutz whose *Der sinnhafte Aufbau der sozialen Welt* of 1932 was not translated into English until 1967 as *The Phenomenology of the Social World* (Schutz, 1967 [1932]). The German title (literally meaning 'the meaningful construction of the social world') better conveys Schutz's view that social constructionism is

---

1. See Robbins (2019, 110) for a more elaborate discussion of this point.

confined to the construction of the world of social relations. He restricted himself to the view that interpersonally people construct the world of social relations within which they live. Bourdieu argued that everything is socially constructed, becoming objectified in various 'fields', including the field of politics. Jürgen Habermas took the view that the world of social relations – civil society – was a historical product, emerging as a consequence of the decline of a particular form of political authority which existed in Western Europe throughout the Middle Ages.

Habermas's *Strukturwandel der Öffentlichkeit* was first published in 1962, and only published in English translation by Massachusetts Institute of Technology Press in the United States and Polity Press in the United Kingdom in 1989 as *The Structural Transformation of the Public Sphere. An Inquiry into a Category of Bourgeois Society*. Habermas begins by characterising the situation in feudal society in Europe in the High Middle Ages as one of 'representative publicness' in which, at the local level, the manorial lord 'displayed himself, presented himself as an embodiment of some sort of "higher" power' (Habermas, 1989, 7). This was a self-representation to a public, replicated in the ceremonial representation of monarchs before their subjects, which had nothing to do with 'Representation in the sense in which the members of a national assembly represent a nation or a lawyer represents his clients' (Habermas, 1989, 7). Habermas proceeds to analyse the breakdown of 'representative publicness' and the consequent 'genesis of the bourgeois public sphere'. He argues that the motor for change was the growth of international trade and the associated 'traffic in news' (Habermas, 1989, 16). Habermas describes the way in which this changed in the following way:

> The bourgeois public sphere may be conceived above all as the sphere of private people come together as a public; they soon claimed the public sphere regulated from above against the public authorities themselves, to engage them in a debate over the general rules governing relations in the basically privatized but publicly relevant sphere of commodity exchange and social labor. The medium of this political confrontation was peculiar and without historical precedent: people's public use of their reason (*öffentliches Räsonnement*). (Habermas, 1989, 27)

Habermas devotes part of chapter III ('Political Functions of the Public Sphere') to the 'model case of British Development' because 'a public sphere that functioned in the political realm arose first in Great Britain at the turn of the eighteenth century' (Habermas, 1989, 57). However, he concludes that this construction of a public sphere, designed to subvert traditional political authority in the interests of a new social group, was not successful in securing its ambition:

> The developed public sphere of civil society was bound up with a complicated constellation of social preconditions. In any event, before long they all changed profoundly, and with their transformation the contradiction of the public sphere that was institutionalized in the bourgeois constitutional state came to the fore. With the help of its principle, which according to its own idea was opposed to all domination, a political order was founded whose social basis did not make domination superfluous after all. (Habermas, 1989, 88)

In his original preface of 1961, Habermas specifically admitted that his research had been restricted to a limited object and had not considered in detail the consequences of the contradictory achievement of this bourgeois revolution of the eighteenth century:

> Our investigation is limited to the structure and function of the *liberal* model of the bourgeois public sphere, to its emergence and transformation. Thus it refers to those features of a historical constellation that attained dominance and leaves aside the *plebeian* public sphere as a variant that in a sense was suppressed in the historical process. (Habermas, 1989, xviii)

He proceeded to acknowledge that a different phenomenon was emerging during the French Revolution, but argues that its conception of a popular public sphere was still conditioned by bourgeois conceptualisation:

> In the stage of the French Revolution associated with Robespierre, for just one moment, a public sphere stripped of its literary garb began to function – its subject was no longer the 'educated strata' but the uneducated 'people'. Yet even this plebeian public sphere whose continued but submerged existence manifested itself in the Chartist Movement and especially in the anarchist traditions of the workers' movement on the continent, remains oriented towards the intentions of the bourgeois public sphere. In the perspective of intellectual history it was, like the latter, a child of the eighteenth century. (Habermas, 1989, xviii)

As a consequence, this emergent 'populism' had nothing in common with the movements which Habermas was observing in his day: 'it must be strictly distinguished from the plebiscitary-acclamatory form of regimented public sphere characterizing dictatorships in highly developed industrial societies'. Fearing both the domination of an uneducated mass and the exploitation of the masses by dictators under the guise of populism, Habermas hints at his future project to encourage the cultivation of a communicatively active, democratic public sphere, one not confined to an intellectual elite:

> Formally they have certain traits in common; but each differs in its own way from the literary character of a public sphere constituted by private people putting reason to use – one is illiterate, the other, after a fashion, post-literary. (Habermas, 1989, xviii)

In short, Habermas recognised that the autonomous social sphere tacitly recommended by Schutz and Goffman was forfeiting its capacity to impinge on a political sphere which was still operating on assumptions derived from the bourgeois appropriation of the representativeness of feudal monarchs.

The intention of this book is to recommend, by example, a retrieval of a plebeian public sphere. By offering six passages written at intervals of about a decade each between 1960 and 2020, it attempts to show the development of an attitude towards politics which has been correlative with the social, intellectual and professional trajectory outlined in short introductions to the passages. This introduction, the conclusion and the six brief introductions all are written in 2020/21. They impose reflexivity retrospectively with a view to communicating the position which is the culmination of the progression expressed in the six passages. That position is that we all need to situate ourselves and each other socially, all recognising the contingency of our career paths and of our relative socio-economic contributions to our societies, and that, to this end, we should resist the tendency of professionalised politics to dominate our language and behaviour. This involves encouraging self-understanding and self-presentation and actively acknowledging that 'representativeness' has become the spurious rationale adopted by politicians to justify their chosen self-presentations. Politics, in other words, is an immanent activity as much as any other, and its aspirations to transcendence need to be resisted as much as all others.

Chapter 1

MR. BENN OR LORD STANSGATE? AN INVESTIGATION OF THE BRISTOL SOUTH-EAST BY-ELECTION, MAY 4, 1961, AND ITS CONSEQUENCES [1962]

A. The Background

I was born in October 1944 in Bristol. I was pre-constituted as a Nonconformist. This is not to say that I was 'naturally' or 'constitutionally' disinclined to conform to authority, but rather that my parents were active members of the local Baptist church. It is strictly inaccurate to call them 'nonconformists'. Historically, protestant denominations were forced to be regarded as such by the attempted imposition, in 1662, of the Act of Uniformity. As David D. Hall has shown recently, this act united, in opposition to the Anglican Church, movements which were fundamentally dissimilar. In particular, the non-conformist label wrongly identified protestants from the reformed tradition with those who were 'separatist'. As early as the 1590s, however, separatists had ceased to try to reform the established church and had, instead, formed congregations of their own. By this means they avoided the two main problems concerning the English Puritans, as identified by Hall:

> The first of these was how to reconcile an inclusive state church with the church as a sanctified community, and the second, how to remain loyal to a Christian prince while acknowledging the authority of divine law. Separatists solved the first by reimagining the visible church as a cluster of small-scale voluntary communities, each of them empowered to exclude the unworthy, and the second by withdrawing from the magistracy-ministry alliance so dear to the Reformed international. (Hall, 2019, 69–70)

As Carlyle wrote in 1845, in his introduction to his edition of *Oliver Cromwell's Letters and Speeches*, the Puritan movement had become 'unintelligible': 'we

understand not even in imagination […] what it ever could have meant'
(Carlyle, 1845, vol. 1, 1–11, quoted in Hall, 2019, 349). This seems even more
so in 2021, but in my childhood I unconsciously imbibed a sense of separateness. The lives of my parents revolved around the local chapel. My father
was a deacon and my mother was a Sunday school teacher. They had no
friends outside the chapel community. There was strict adherence to Lord's
Day Observance on Sundays and also to total abstinence from alcohol. There
was no television in the house until well after the queen's coronation in 1952.
I remember no conversation at all about politics. We took the *News Chronicle*
until it ceased in October 1960, which suggests sympathies with the Liberal
Party, but I had no knowledge of this orientation. As a family, we had very
short holidays each year locally – either in the South-West or in Wales. As
a child, I studied for exams of the Scripture Union and, as a teenager, I was
involved in events and holidays organised for youth groups by the Bristol
Baptist churches and the Baptist Union.

In the second half of the nineteenth century, the Broad Church Movement
waged a campaign against Nonconformists with a view to restoring the unity
of the Anglican Church. Matthew Arnold depicted Nonconformists as uncul-
tured and materialist, associated with industrialisation and commercialisation.
For him, the values of Nonconformism were antipathetic to the 'sweetness
and light' that he recommended in his culture. 'Look at the life imaged in
such a newspaper as the *Nonconformist*', he wrote, '- a life of jealousy of the
Establishment, disputes, tea-meetings, openings of chapels, sermons; …'
(Arnold, 1963 [1869], 58).

This did not correspond with my experience. I had no sense of deprivation
nor of exclusion. I had simply inherited a quiet, confident sense of differentness. I attended the local primary school and my mother encouraged my
reading and writing. I won a scholarship to Bristol Grammar School preparatory school, starting just before I was 8 years old in September 1952. I passed
the 11+ exam and moved on to the Upper School in the autumn of 1956.
There were no boarders, but it felt like a total institution in that school attendance was for six days each week, with sport on Saturday afternoons. Apart
from some youth activities, my whole life was dominated by school and home-
work during the week and by church attendance on Sundays. There were two
significant curricular choices at school. The first was that at about the age of
14 I chose to learn German rather than Greek. This put me on course for
entry to the 'Modern' rather than the 'Classical' sixth form. I started to study
three subjects for 'A'-level in 1960. These were English, French and History,
and I continued to study Latin in order to make entrance possible to either
Oxford or Cambridge. I particularly remember two of the set texts in English
literature. These were the first two books of Milton's *Paradise Lost* and the first

two books of Wordsworth's *The Prelude*. I think I am not reading too much into my response to these texts when I say that Milton's poem transformed my understanding of the Bible, causing me to see a theological narrative politically as epitomising a tension between free will and determinism; and when I say that Wordsworth's autobiographical epic encouraged me to consider self-development as the consequence of affective as much as of intellectual influence. Nevertheless, even at that time, I was drawn to the work of Coleridge, as an intellectual, more than to that of Wordsworth. The specifics of the history curriculum were also important. The syllabus involved the study of English and continental history from 1600 to 1800. In the former, I was particularly engaged by study of the English Civil War, and, in the latter, by study of the French Revolution. In both cases, the analyses of popular revolts against aristocratic privilege supplied some kind of objective correlative to my own situation, having the effect of enabling me for the first time to see my social differentness as the historical product of political and class exclusion. This lies in the background to my choice of the project which led to the report reproduced in this chapter.

I took my 'A'-level examinations in the spring of 1962. I carried out research for a submission for a Trevelyan Scholarship between April and July 1962, when I must have been waiting for my results. I have no recollection of how the suggestion arose that I should submit a report for this funding nor how I chose the topic. I suspect that there were two influences. Firstly, I had been interested within the History syllabus in the succession of expulsions and re-elections to parliament of John Wilkes in Middlesex elections in 1769. He had championed the rights of his voters, rather than the House of Commons, to determine their representatives. There seemed to be a parallel with the expulsion of Anthony Wedgwood Benn from his parliamentary seat in Bristol South East a year before, and there was the additional appeal that the recent conflict accentuated a challenge to inherited privilege. Secondly, I had been a member, since its inception, of a school society which was launched in the early 1960s by two young members of staff. Called *Thorn*, it introduced students to social research and, in particular, carried out and published an analysis of the social class distribution of boys at the school, modelled on Jackson and Marsden's recently published *Education and the Working Class* (Jackson and Marsden, 1962). In short, these factors caused me to undertake an analysis of the voting behaviour in a constituency near my home, an analysis which was an uncertain mixture of contemporary history and sociology. My growing awareness of social inequalities led, for the first time, to a *political* enquiry.

The report on my enquiry into the Bristol South East by-election of May 1961, issued as *Mr. Benn or Lord Stansgate?*, was the result of research in Keesing's Contemporary Archives and back numbers of local newspapers;

interviews with the two candidates and their agents; background reading; and tabulation of voting statistics. Its methodological naiveté is a reflection of my inexperience and also of the underdevelopment of political science at the time. The report cites three of the 'Nuffield' election surveys – those of the British General Elections of 1951 (Butler, 1952), 1955 (Butler, 1955) and 1959 (Butler and Rose, 1960), and it quotes from R. S. Milne and H. C. Mackenzie, *Marginal Seat, 1955* (Milne and Mackenzie, 1958), which, as its subtitle specifies, was 'a study of voting behaviour in the constituency of Bristol North-East at the General Election of 1955'.

Not referenced is Butler's *The Study of Political Behaviour* (Butler, 1958) which studied various approaches to political analysis and presented his view of the contemporary situation. Born in 1924, Butler studied Philosophy, Politics and Economics (PPE) at New College, Oxford, where his tutor was Sir Isaiah Berlin. His studies were interrupted by the war, but he produced a statistical model for analysing elections which was appended to the first Nuffield Election study in 1947 (McCallum and Readman, 1947). He spent 1947–48 in the United States carrying out research at Princeton University on opinion polls and following the candidates in the presidential election of November 1948. In 1949–51 he wrote a DPhil thesis at Nuffield College, Oxford, which was published in 1953 (Butler, 1953). Butler's survey of the field of study of 1958 reflected his PPE training and his absorption of American empirical procedures. In an introductory chapter on the 'nature of the subject', Butler emphasises that his book is 'entitled *The Study of Political Behaviour* and not the *Study of Politics*' (Butler, 1958, 15). He deliberately avoids defining 'politics', but he continues that 'politics is entirely concerned with people, with the way in which they make decisions and with the way in which they react to decisions' (Butler, 1958, 15). He insists, in other words, that 'politics' is not to be understood as a system which is independent of social practices. However, he proceeds to represent a range of ways in which politics can be studied. He gives an account of 'the deductive approach' which follows from a priori political philosophy; the 'descriptive approach' which is historical; 'the quantitative approach' which is statistical; and 'the sociological and psychological approach' which is pertinent because 'sociologists, anthropologists, and psychologists are all concerned with the study of man's activities and attitudes and necessarily include some aspects of politics within their purview' (Butler, 1958, 76). He concludes with a consideration of 'the practical approach', followed by a summary of the 'possibilities and limits' for the study of political behaviour. He comments that 'what is required is a spirit of constructive criticism enlisting all the approaches described in the preceding chapters' (Butler, 1958, 106).

R. B. McCallum was a history fellow (later master) at Pembroke College, Oxford. He encouraged the study of elections, wrote a significant account of 'The study of psephology' (a word which he coined) in 1954 (McCallum, 1954), but his approach was always historical. Robert S. Milne (1919–2014) was a lecturer in government in the Economics department at the University of Bristol, and H. C. Mackenzie was a statistician in the same department. Milne and Mackenzie wrote a book about the General Election of 1951 in the Bristol North East Bristol constituency, published in 1954 (Milne and Mackenzie, 1954) in which they indicated that they had undertaken their research because they believed that the Nuffield College election studies 'needed to be supplemented by detailed studies of voting behaviour designed to discover "what makes the elector tick"' (Milne and Mackenzie, 1954, 7). In their introduction, they distinguished between two broad classes of electoral study – those focusing on what political parties do at elections and those concentrating on 'individual voters, usually in a single constituency' (Milne and Mackenzie, 1954, 10). Both *Straight Fight* and *Marginal Seat* were attempts to undertake analysis of the second kind. As precedents, they cited separate surveys of 1950 carried out by staff at the London School of Economics and Political Science (LSE) and at the University of Manchester, published in the *British Journal of Sociology*[1] in 1950 (Benney and Geiss, 1950; Birch and Campbell, 1950), but they acknowledged that these studies were primarily influenced by the survey of the American presidential election of 1940 undertaken by Paul Lazarsfeld, published as *The People's Choice* (Lazarsfeld, Berelson and Gaudet, 1948).

A. H. Halsey's *A History of Sociology in Britain* (Halsey, 2004) highlights the impact on the development of the discipline of the diffusion of graduates from the LSE into new departments of sociology in the United Kingdom from the mid-1950s. He lists 13 people who graduated between 1950 and 1952, and he comments: 'Most, if not all, had 'won the scholarship'. There was only one woman (Olive Banks). There were no 'public' school boys among them' (Halsey, 2004, 73). I was the product of a grammar school and, in 1963, was to win a scholarship to study at Cambridge. At that date, my school still regarded the success of its students in Oxbridge entrance as the primary measure of its achievement. It was inconceivable that I should aspire to seek admission at any other university and, of course, neither Cambridge nor Oxford formally recognised the existence of sociology. In spite of the references to voting figures, which are rather descriptive than the bases for statistical analysis, my report shows that I had inclinations, in Butler's terms, towards the 'sociological and psychological' approach to politics as opposed to the historical approach

---

1. The first number of the *British Journal of Sociology*, edited by M. Ginsberg, D. V. Glass and T. H. Marshall, appeared in March 1950.

which I had acquired in my 'A'-level work. This inclination remained dormant as I sought entry to Cambridge to read English literature.

B. The Text

I

The first Viscount Stansgate died on 17 November 1960, and the title passed to his son, Anthony Wedgwood Benn, Labour MP for Bristol South East. In 1955, the Viscount had presented a Bill which would allow the peerage to be in abeyance during his son's lifetime, but this had been rejected. Would Benn now accept the peerage, or would he return to the constitutional struggle?

On November 23 Benn announced that he had executed an instrument of renunciation, symbolised by the return of the letters patent to the Lord Chamberlain. At the same time he planned to petition the House of Commons to consider three new legal arguments which he hoped would enable him to remain a commoner. He claimed that

a. This was the first action of its kind since 1678 when it was forbidden for reasons which are now obsolete.
b. A peerage is 'a place' and not 'an office', and therefore he could not be disqualified under the 1957 House of Commons Disqualification Act.[2]
c. The Crown had no right by prerogative to prevent a member from taking his seat in the Commons.

The Tuesday after, November 29, Sir Lynn Ungoed-Thomas, QC (Labour) presented a petition by Benn in the House of Commons which submitted that he 'is and should remain' a Member of the House for as long as he might be elected. The House decided to refer the Petition to the Committee of Privileges, and consequently all further discussion within Parliament was delayed until after this Committee had reached its conclusions. Meanwhile, Benn was supremely hopeful that he would remain a member of the House of Commons. Before the death of his father, he said, he would not have put his chances of renouncing his peerage at 2 per cent. 'But since then I have been staggered at the offers of support and sympathetic letters. The backing is tremendous.'[3] However, much of his confidence was broken when the Committee of Privileges reached its decision.

---

2. Keesing's Contemporary Archives, p. 16189, 2nd col., p. 14381 A.
3. Reported in the *Bristol Evening Post*, 22 November 1960.

On 21 March 1961, the Committee, under the chairmanship of Mr R. A. Butler, Home Secretary and Leader of the House, and comprising 14 members drawn from the Conservative, Labour, and Liberal parties, eventually, after 11 meetings, rejected Benn's Petition. It reached six conclusions of which the most important was that 'Mr. Wedgwood Benn was disqualified from membership of the Commons on November 17th, 1960, by succession to the Viscounty of Stansgate'.

Three days later, Sir Lynn Ungoed-Thomas introduced the Peerage (Renunciation) Bill which included a clause: 'Any person who has executed an instrument of renunciation in accordance with the provisions of this Act shall, if elected, enjoy the same rights to sit and vote as a member of the House of Commons as any other commoner.' Four Conservative members backed the Bill and consequently on March 29 they resented Mr Butler's statement that the Whips would be put on for the forthcoming debate on the decision of the Committee of Privileges. This debate was scheduled for April 13, and on the 12 every Conservative MP received a reproduction of a letter which Sir Winston Churchill had written in support of Benn's case in 1955. Meanwhile, Mr Wilkins, Labour MP for Bristol South presented a petition signed by 10,357 electors in the Bristol South East constituency asking Parliament to allow Benn to remain their member.

Yet these efforts had little effect on the decisions of the House the next day. In an editorial on April 13, the *Bristol Evening Post* commented: 'We have found only slender grounds for hoping that pointless traditionalism in Parliament will have given way to enlightened common sense by 10 o'clock to-night.' To the disappointment of Benn it was proved right. Firstly, the Speaker (Sir Harry Hylton-Foster) reported that he had received a letter from Benn asking that he should be allowed to address the House from the Bar on the subject of the Committee of Privileges' report. The Leader of the Opposition then moved: 'That Mr. Wedgwood Benn be admitted and heard'. Mr Gaitskell appealed to historical precedent[4] and asserted that to his knowledge 'there is no single case in the history of the House of Commons where a member whose right to sit is in dispute and who has asked leave to address the House, has been refused'. Nevertheless, the motion was rejected after debate by 221 votes to 152 – a government majority of 69.

Mr Butler then moved: 'That this House takes note of the fact that Mr. Anthony Neil Wedgwood Benn on succession to the Viscounty of Stansgate on November 17, 1960, ceased to be a member of this House, and agrees with the Committee of Privileges in its report.' The leader of the Opposition then moved the following amendment to the government's motion: 'That

---

4. Three precedents: Daniel O'Connell, Charles Bradlaugh, Rev. J. G. MacManaway.

legislation should be introduced forthwith to provide for the renunciation of peerages and to allow those who have renounced a peerage to vote in and to be candidates at parliamentary elections and, if elected, to be members of the Commons House of Parliament'. The Opposition's amendment was rejected by 207 votes to 143 (government majority of 64) and the government's motion adopted by 204–126 (government majority of 78).

The Opposition amendment was supported by the Liberals and by 10 to 15 Conservative back-benchers, but this was small consolation for the fact that the House of Commons had emphatically rejected Benn's renunciation of the peerage. The decisions in the House on April 13 necessitated a by-election, and so the 'reluctant peer' prepared to present his case before an electorate. On the application of Mr Herbert Bowden, Opposition Chief Whip, the Speaker issued a parliamentary writ on April 18. Attention swung rapidly from Westminster to the South-East of Bristol, the city which once did itself the honour of electing the great campaigner Edmund Burke to Parliament. What kind of constituency was it that Benn was later to call his 'secret weapon'?[5]

II

'Bristol has for the first time in its history given openings to Labour-Socialism by the victories of Mr. W. J. Baker in the East and Mr. W. H. Ayles in the North' reported the Bristol Times and Mirror in disgust on 7 December 1923. Bristol East, as the constituency was then, was therefore in the forefront of the Labour movement in Bristol, and it has remained so ever since. In the General Elections of 1924 and 1929, Mr Baker's majority increased so that after his death, Bristol East was considered a safe seat in which to place the newly appointed solicitor general, Sir Richard Stafford Cripps. At the by-election on 16 January 1931, Cripps was returned with an overall majority of 7,314 votes. On August 28, he resigned[6] from the National Government which Stanley Baldwin and Ramsay MacDonald had engineered, but such was the strength of the Labour movement in the constituency that in the General Election in October of the same year, Cripps retained his seat, the sole Labour member to survive in the South of England outside London.[7] After the landslide of 1931, Sir Stafford Cripps gradually increased his majority just as the Labour Party gradually recovered its political influence. But in 1950, Sir Stafford was forced to retire through ill-health. As he had initially been an unpopular

5. Reported in the *Bristol Evening Post*, 22 April 1961.
6. C. Cooke, 1957, *The life of Richard Stafford Cripps*, London: Hodder & Stoughton, 126.
7. Cooke (1957, 136).

choice[8], so with his successor, Anthony Wedgwood Benn. The new candidate was returned in November with a decreased, but still substantial majority. In the General Election of 1951, Benn almost doubled this majority, but since, in 1955 and again in 1959 there has been an apparent swing towards the Tories.

However, it is not so much the constituents as the actual local Labour Party that has influenced the history of Bristol East, and subsequently of Bristol South East. The constituency party has always possessed a strong sense of independence combined with deep loyalty to its elected MP. On 25 January 1939, Sir Stafford Cripps was expelled from the labour Party, but was immediately given a vote of confidence[9] by the local party. There followed a split in the party of Bristol East with the result that many who continued to support their MP were expelled from the constituency Labour Party. There were thus two Labour parties in Bristol East: an unofficial one supporting the member, and an official one consisting of many staunch Trade-unionists, which was not sure of its attitude to Sir Stafford. These divided loyalties were only reunited in March 1945, when Sir Stafford was formally readmitted to the National Executive which had expelled him.[10] The whole episode shows how many members of the constituency Labour Party felt that it was more important to remain loyal to the man whom they had grown to admire, than to obey the instructions of their national party. It is not unreasonable to suggest that the stubborn loyalty and love of independence shown between 1939 and 1945 were present once more when the local party opposed Benn's expulsion from the House of Commons.

It was, therefore, 'in character' for the Labour Party of Bristol South East to enjoy supporting Benn against tradition, yet the Labour vote was not the deciding factor in the poll. In his election report, the Labour agent, Mr Herbert Rogers, writes: 'There can be little doubt that some Liberals and maybe those who had previously voted Conservative, voted for Benn this time. I would say that the many Tory abstentions were a protest against the action of the Government in preventing Tony Benn from remaining in the House of Commons.'

The Liberals were of unknown numerical strength within the constituency. They had fought the seat twice in 1950 and had gained 4,463 votes in February and 2,752 in November. Mr Christopher Pym at one time proposed to fight the by-election as a Liberal candidate, but his fate suggests that if they voted, the Liberals of the constituency would almost certainly have been in sympathy with Benn. On January 1, Mr Pym offered himself as a potential candidate for the constituency, but it was reported in the *Evening Post* of January 23 that

---

8. Cooke (1957, 114).
9. Cooke (1957, 236).
10. Cooke (1957, 324).

Lady Violet Bonham Carter had advised all Bristol Liberals to help Benn, and that, consequently, he had withdrawn his offer. Although Mr Pym then decided to oppose Benn as an independent[11] (a decision which circumstances later forced him to withdraw[12]), the regional Liberal Party did not vacillate. It issued the following statement on April 4: 'If Mr. Benn is allowed to stand in the forth-coming by-election in Bristol South-East, and if he fights the election on the constitutional issue, Liberals will not oppose him, but they consider in the circumstances, that he should be well advised to stand as an independent and limit his campaign to the constitutional position.' If the few Liberals in the constituency voted, they must have voted for Benn, but it is impossible to decide whether in comparison to previous elections these voters would only appear as Conservative abstentions, since, for lack of a Liberal candidate, the Liberals probably had voted Conservative.

After his defeat in the General Election of 26 May 1955, Mr Robert Cooke (Conservative) stated: 'We have got the highest Tory vote we have ever had in what is a Labour seat, although it is a lower poll. It has never been a Conservative seat, but in Bristol South-East our vote has gone up and up.' In fact there had been a larger Tory vote in 1931, but Mr Cooke was right in that the Conservative vote had been increasing recently. The swing to the Conservatives in the constituency during the '50s can partly be attributed to the redistribution of the wards between 1951 and 1955. Bristol South East lost Labour strongholds such as St. Philip's Marsh where 1,100 of the 1,300 electors could be guaranteed to vote Labour, whilst it gained two wards which were not so strongly Labour, although they both had 100 per cent Labour representation on the Town Council. However, if this explains why the Conservatives gained in strength between 1951 and 1955, it cannot explain why the trend continued.

Thus, when Benn turned his attention more specifically towards Bristol on April 18, he could be pleased that he was going to a constituency with a history of staunch support for the labour movement. Yet, at the same time, he would have been foolish to forget that his majority in this very constituency had steadily decreased since 1951.

III

Wedgwood Benn and his opponent, Malcolm St Clair, handed in their nomination papers on April 24. Both candidates were young and consequently the short campaign was to be energetically contested. Benn had an impressive

---

11. Reported in the *Bristol Evening Post*, 22 March 1961.
12. Reported in the *Bristol Evening Post*, 26 April 1961.

record behind him both before he entered the Commons and whilst there[13]; St Clair was represented as the Tetbury farmer.[14] The Conservative candidate worked very hard, yet Benn worked just a little harder. In articles in the *Evening Post* a day in the life of each candidate was described.[15] St Clair attempted to include four hours of canvassing in his day, whereas Benn attempted six hours. Benn was called the 'human dynamo'[16] and was known to be a man of zest and talent. St Clair was hard-working but uninspiring.

Under the candidates (who may only sway at the most 1,000 voters[17]) both parties had efficient organizations. The Conservatives were helped by Mr Rex Bagnall from Central Office; Mr Bryan Little, the author; Mr Geoffrey Newman; and Mr Fred Moores, the agent for Bristol North East. The agent for the constituency was Colonel Moggridge who had only been agent for four years. The Labour Party in Bristol South East received assistance from the regional office and especially from the regional secretary, Mr Red Rees. Mr Percy Clark, an expert from Transport House, directed publicity. Their only advantage lay in the experience of their agent, Mr Rogers, who had been actively connected with the constituency for over forty years.

The deciding factor in the election was the enthusiasm of Benn's supporters and helpers. This was apparent in their canvassing. Help was received from the Liberals, the Exeter and Tiverton divisions, the Bath Young Socialists, and also from some University students. Consequently, at least 40 per cent of every ward was canvassed, and in Hanham Ward a 95 per cent canvas was accomplished. In comparison, after the election, St Clair admitted that he had canvassed 30 per cent of the constituency over the last four years. With only 60 volunteer helpers, the Conservatives relied on the canvassing of previous years which, of course, had not involved the special issue of a disqualified candidate. On the other hand, as a result of the constituency petition and of Benn's canvassing, there were very few people who were not aware of the Labour attitude to the issue at stake in the by-election.

The contrasting impressions of vigour and dullness were maintained by the party meetings. Benn had said: 'The campaign will turn into a two-week summer school of some of the most exciting, most intelligent and most useful people in Britain to-day,'[18] and this was no vain promise. St Clair stubbornly reiterated that he was fighting the election strictly on the Tory record and

---

13. See *Who's Who 1962*, London: Adam and Charles Black, 1962, 223.
14. See Ibid., 2685.
15. The *Bristol Evening Post*, St Clair: 27 April 1961. Benn: 28 April 1961.
16. The *Bristol Evening Post*, 28 April 1961.
17. R. S. Milne and H. C. Mackenzie, *Marginal Seat*, 1955, 158.
18. Reported in the *Bristol Evening Post*, 19 April 1961.

he invited few speakers other than the local Tory MPs, except for some legal experts. The Tories held one meeting every evening except on Sundays, and on the eve of the poll they held three. Benn held 26 meetings in 10 days (between April 24 and May 3). Not only did the Tories hold fewer meetings but in general these were less well attended than those of the Labour Party. This is not surprising when the electors had to choose between Jo Grimond MP, Anthony Crosland MP, Fenner Brockway MP or Robert Cooke (Conservative MP for Bristol West) on April 25; Michael Foot MP or Alan Hopkins (Conservative MP for Bristol North East) on April 26; Dr Donald Soper, Mr James Cameron or John Peyton (Conservative MP for Yeovil) on April 27. The Tories had a few spectacular meetings such as when Mr Butler, Sir Lionel Heald or Sir Edward Boyle spoke, but otherwise their meetings were not likely to attract the uncommitted elector. The *Evening Post* says of one Conservative meeting: 'Last night a dozen people turned up, nobody felt like asking questions, and all was over in half an hour.'[19] The Conservative meetings had poor attendances, yet, such is the apathy of the British electorate, that in spite of excellent speakers, the Labour meetings were not well attended, averaging at about forty to fifty people. But Benn gained the largest audience of the campaign in an open air meeting on the eve of the poll when he addressed a crowd of nearly five hundred.

In all of these meetings, as in all of the campaign, there was the one central issue. Judging by the space used in the *Evening Post* in reporting the election meetings, 75 per cent of the Labour meetings was devoted to discussion of the constitutional problem in comparison to 60 per cent of the Conservative meetings. But it was his treatment of the problem that gained Benn support. St Clair tried to isolate the issue, whereas Benn showed that tradition was the root cause of the wrongs of English society. A vote for Benn would be a blow against the tradition which had forced him to lose his seat in the House of Commons. St Clair attempted to pull Benn away from his progressive platform and to restrict him to party politics. The Conservative challenged his opponent to reveal his attitude on defence in the hope that this would split the Labour voters, but Benn ignored the challenge. Benn maintained that the constitutional issue had necessitated the by-election and that therefore he would make it decide the result.

Only a small minority of the voters attend the public meetings, while the rest are influenced during the campaign by the mass media or propaganda. Neither of the candidates was able to find much space for posters, although the local Co-operative Society allowed the Labour Party to use some of its advertising

---

19. The *Bristol Evening Post*, 27 April 1961.

space. The candidates probably concentrated their greatest efforts on printing and distributing literature. For Benn, it was always of primary importance that he should win the by-election, and his literature was directed to this end. The petition showed the electorate what Benn was attempting to do, and this was re-emphasized in the election address. St Clair refused to mention Benn in his election address, treating the election as if his opponent was nothing other than an ordinary Labour candidate. Although he never admitted the fact, it became clear that St Clair's main consideration was the Election Court rather than the election. He attacked Benn's legal position by publishing a document, addressed to the Electors of the Bristol South East Constituency, containing the words, 'Now take Notice, that all votes given for the said Anthony Neil Wedgwood Benn, second Viscount Stansgate of Stansgate, at the said election will by reason of the said incapacity and disqualification be thrown away, and be null and void.' This notice was widely distributed, appearing in the local papers and on posters outside the polling stations. St Clair was wise, on the long term, to make this move, for it was mainly on this evidence that the Election Court was to reach its decision. Benn's response was swift and effective. Referring to the Tory move, Benn said: 'They are planning to post their phoney legal message on polling stations in a desperate last minute attempt to frighten away those people who are going to vote according to their conscience for the can-didate of their choice.'[20] St Clair's claim that votes cast for Benn were wasted votes was used to increase support for Labour by such slogans: 'Don't be misled by Tory Red Herrings, Every Vote for Benn will count on Thursday. Don't let the Tory in by the Back Door.'

Away from the legal conflict, Benn was steadily winning more support. On April 21 he produced the first edition of the *Bristol Campaigner* which was intended to tell his supporters of the latest developments in the campaign, and to advise them on what they should do. Twelve editions appeared, cre-ating a strong informed body of opinion within the Labour Party and a united front to opposition. In issue no. 8 on Sunday, April 30, there were notes for party workers and canvassers which explained how they should deal with St Clair's 'phoney legal document' if the matter should arise at meetings or during canvassing. Issue no. 9, on the next day, encouraged his supporters by showing the results of a Gallup Poll conducted by the *Daily Telegraph*. It also contained letters of exhortation from supporters elsewhere and it underlined the fact that many Tories in the rest of the country were supporting Benn. The 'Bristol Campaigner' was mainly directed at the Labour worker and it only angled hopefully for the Conservative elector. Then, two days from polling,

---

20. Reported in the *Bristol Evening Post*, 3 May 1961.

Benn launched his surprise attack on the Conservative sections of the constituency. A total of 10,000 copies of Sir Winston Churchill's letter of support written in 1953 were distributed. The move was well-timed since St Clair was unable to counteract the effect that this letter might have in Tory circles. As it was, he could only make the wry comment: 'Surely it would have been more in keeping had he received support from his former leader, Mr. Atlee.'[21]

Amidst the publicity which Benn was zealously giving himself, he was also receiving plenty from the press. At the beginning of the campaign, the *Evening Post* commented in an editorial: 'Mr. Benn and Mr. St. Clair will have their own themes. We shall not, of course, take sides.'[22] Yet, in spite of this assertion of political neutrality, by supporting Benn in his constitutional struggle, the paper effectively helped him in his campaign. The *Evening Post* has the widest circulation, and the other local papers, the *Western Daily Press* and the *Bristol Evening World* were also sympathetic to Benn's cause.

In the early hours of May 5, the result of the by-election was declared:

A. N. Wedgwood Benn (Labour)	23, 275
M.A. St. Clair (Conservative)	10, 231

Benn's majority of 13, 044 was more than double the majority he had gained over the same opponent in the General Election of 1959. In comparison to that election, 56.2 per cent of the electorate recorded their votes against 81.36 per cent, the Labour vote fell by 2,998, and the Conservative vote by 10, 215. '56.2% is a good percentage poll for a by-election, bearing in mind that it rained all through polling day' – 'The swing away from the Tories was even greater at Worcester.' These arguments attempt to detract from Benn's achievement. The combination of a low percentage poll and of a great decline in the Tory vote suggests that Benn's campaign had caused many Tory abstentions. On May 8, Mr Wilkins (Labour MP for Bristol South) drew on what he had witnessed during the campaign to make the following statement before the House of Commons: 'I do not believe that the whole of the 10,000 Conservatives who apparently failed to vote necessarily abstained. I have very good evidence for saying that. If I had to suggest some proportion I should say that probably there were nearer 7,000 or 8,000 abstentions, and that 2,000 or 3,000 Conservatives actually voted for Mr. Wedgwood Benn.'[23] He then gave two examples which demonstrated his opinion. The polling

---

21. Reported in the *Bristol Evening Post*, 2 May 1961.
22. The *Bristol Evening Post*, 19 April 1961.
23. Hansard Volume 640, No. 105, col. 110, 8 May 1961.

figures at the various stations suggest the same conclusion. In Hanham, a very strong Labour area, the percentage vote was down by 20 per cent, whilst in Stockwood, a more Tory district, the percentage vote was down by 30 per cent.[24] The energy and drive which Benn displayed throughout the campaign had forced Conservatives into sympathy, and made them unwilling to go out into the rain to support their own dull candidate.

Benn had won a great victory and deserved the acclaim which he received in the constituency, but he had defeated a man who could afford to lose, he had temporarily defeated a man who was working for ultimate success.

IV

On May 8, Benn presented himself at the House of Commons, but, on the instructions of the Speaker, the Principal Doorkeeper refused him admission. Within the House, the Leader of the Opposition moved: 'That Mr. Anthony Neil Wedgwood Benn be admitted in and heard'. After debate, Mr Gaitskell's motion was rejected by 250 votes to 177. Mr Butler then moved:

> That this House, taking note that Mr. Anthony Neil Wedgwood Benn ceased to be a member of this House on succession to the Viscounty of Stansgate on November 17th, 1960, and that a new writ was issued for the election of a member in the room of the said Anthony Neil Wedgwood Benn, orders that the said Anthony Neil Wedgwood Benn, otherwise Viscount Stansgate, be not permitted to enter the Chamber unless the House otherwise orders.

Mr George Brown (Labour) then moved an amendment to make the motion read: 'That this House, taking note that the electors of South-East Bristol have returned Mr. Anthony Neil Wedgwood Benn as their member, resolves that, notwithstanding the resolution of this House on April 13th, the oath be administered to Mr. Anthony Neil Wedgwood Benn, and that he do take his seat.'

The Opposition amendment was rejected by 259 to 162, after which the government's motion was carried by 254 votes to 160. The day followed the same pattern as on April 13, but it must have been more disheartening for Benn. The government's majority had been four less in April in deciding that he should not be heard at the Bar, and the government's motion was adopted now with a greater majority in spite of the fact that in the meantime Benn had gained an overwhelming vote of confidence from his constituency.

---

24. Election report of the Labour agent.

On the same day, May 8, St Clair and an elector of the constituency presented in the Queen's Bench Division a petition asking the Election Court to determine the validity of Benn's election as the Member for Bristol South East. The case opened before the Court of Queen's Bench on July 10, and was heard before Mr Justice Gorman and Mr Justice McNair. St Clair was represented by Sir Andrew Clark, QC, while Benn conducted his own case. The decision of the Court was reached on July 28 that Benn had not been duly elected or returned, and that therefore they had to declare St Clair duly elected. Three days later a motion that the Clerk of the Crown should amend the roll of members by substituting St Clair's name for Benn's was carried in the House of Commons by 235 votes to 145, and consequently St Clair took his seat.

When St Clair entered to take the oath, the majority of the Labour members present left the Chamber. Thus the Labour members had made a gesture of disapproval just as the electors of Bristol South-East had made a 'noble gesture', but had the gestures and the sympathy brought any solid achievement? On July 31, the answer might have suggested that the whole struggle had been a failure, yet, in fact, in the midst of the arguments over precedents, Benn had gained the crucial victory.

Throughout, Tory sympathy for Benn had been strong, but the predominant feeling was always, 'The only way to get a change is to alter the existing law [...] The decision of the electors of South-East Bristol does not alter the existing legal position.'[25] On April 13, Mr Butler had said: 'The Government do not exclude the possibility of future reform of the House of Lords. Indeed, during debate on the Life Peerages Bill – I introduced the second reading – it was mentioned both here and in another place that such a possibility was not remote but was indeed a definite possibility.'[26] Shortly before the by-election in Bristol South East, Mr Butler informed the House of Commons of the government's intention to appoint a joint select committee of both Houses of Parliament to consider reforms in the composition of the House of Lords. He said that its terms of reference would be

To consider, having regard among other things to the need to maintain an efficient Second Chamber:

---

25. The Attorney-General (Sir Reginald Manningham-Buller), Hansard Volume 640, No. 105, col. 162, col. 164, 8 May 1961. Keesing's Contemporary Archives, p. 18089. Col. 1.
26. Hansard vol. 638, No. 88, col. 570, 13 April 1961. Keesing's Contemporary Archives, p. 18086, col. 2.

a. The composition of the House of Lords;
b. Whether any, and if so what, changes should be made in the rights of peers and peeresses in their own right in regard to eligibility to sit in either House of Parliament and to vote at parliamentary elections; and whether any, and if so what, changes should be made in the law relating to the surrender of peerages;
c. Whether it would be desirable to introduce the principle of remuneration for members of the House of Lords, and if so, subject to what conditions, and to make recommendations.

The joint select committee is still sitting.

What does this mean for Bristol South East?

By anticipating the result of the by-election, Mr Butler attempted to give the impression that the government's action was unforced, and his astuteness seems to destroy the significance of the Bristol South East by-election. Yet, even if the mechanism for reform was set in motion before the constituents went to the polling booths, the votes they recorded impressed the House of Commons in May, 1961, and will always provide an interesting example of the strength of public opinion.

What does this mean for Benn?

After the appointment of the joint select committee, Mr Gaitskell said: 'I believe this constitutes a victory for Mr. Benn. It would certainly not have happened had it not been for the struggle he put up to remove the sons of peers from their present disabilities.'[27]

Will the joint select committee reach a decision that will allow Benn to sit in the House of Commons?

Will Benn, in the end, emerge triumphant from his struggle?

---

27. Keesing's Contemporary Archives, p. 18089, col. 2.

Chapter 2

1795: THE POLITICAL LECTURES [1972]

A. The Background

My interviews with the candidates and their agents for 'Mr. Benn or Lord Stansgate?' took place in July 1962. I must have submitted the report at the end of the month. At about the same time, I received my A-level results and, as expected, stayed on at school for a third year in the sixth form in order to sit Oxbridge entrance examinations. I took the Cambridge entrance examinations in a freezing Cambridge in December 1962. After receiving an offer of a place at Clare College to read English, I left school at the end of the second term of that school year, at Easter, 1963. I heard at the beginning of January that my Trevelyan scholarship application had not been successful. There were some moderate signs of subversion in my last years at school. I was among the few prefects who caused some stir in the school by wearing a CND (Campaign for Nuclear Disarmament) badge on school uniform, and I won the annual public speaking competition with a speech which satirically imitated the accent of Harold Macmillan and joked about the policies of his government. The decision to study the electoral process by which Tony Benn sought to renounce his peerage in order to remain an MP was consistent with these anti-establishment demonstrations. The positions adopted were not articulated politically. They simply indicated an underlying moral objection to militarism and to class distinctions. They may also disclose a tension between an inherited framework of moral obligation and a desire to develop and express independent attitudes. It was, perhaps, a wish to explore that tension which caused me to leave school and to spend three months in the spring of 1963 working in a market garden in Vallentuna, near Stockholm, in Sweden. I learnt Swedish, read Strindberg and the whole of Shakespeare, but also observed the ambivalent puritanism and permissiveness of Swedish society.

I started at Clare College just one week before my 19th birthday. I have written elsewhere about the differences of 'cultural capital' between students studying English at Clare (and the whole university), dependent on their previous schooling.[1] I was conscious of becoming initiated into a discourse. By the end of the three years I had become proficient. Academic success was my main goal. I simply assumed that this was why I was there. My social life revolved around the college and several university societies – the Student Christian Movement, the Baptist society and the Film society. I had no involvement at all with student politics. The three-year degree involved immersion in literary texts, from middle English onwards, but I took advantage of the open lecture system to attend lectures in other faculties, such as moral sciences and divinity. These enabled me to pursue an interest in what the English Faculty then called literature and 'its background'. I took advantage of an opportunity provided by the English Faculty to submit small projects alongside Part I and Part II examinations, in 1965 and 1966. The first was a short consideration of the experiments of Southey and Coleridge with 'laughing gas' at the Hot Well in Bristol in the early 1790s, and the second was a longer analysis of the relations between emergent science and technology and traditional culture in Cornwall in the eighteenth century (when it was in the vanguard of the Industrial Revolution because of its tin mines). These were preparatory to my application, in 1966, to continue study for a PhD.

The system only required a short synopsis of my research project by way of formal application. I proposed to study 'literature and science, 1770–1800, with special reference to Joseph Priestley and Samuel Taylor Coleridge'. I was assigned to Raymond Williams[2] as my director of studies, and supplementary supervision was arranged with Professor Mary Hesse[3] and Dr Robert Young,[4] both of the newly established Department of the History and Philosophy of Science. As an undergraduate I had followed the 'Two Cultures' debate between C. P. Snow and F. R. Leavis,[5] and I had also listened to lectures given by some of the main proponents of the Cambridge 'new theology' of the period who were instrumental in introducing to the English intellectual

---

1. Robbins (2010).
2. Raymond Williams (1921–1988), at that time, most known for *Culture and Society* (1958) and *The Long Revolution* (1961). Having received his MA at Cambridge in 1946, Williams returned to Cambridge in 1961, becoming a reader in 1967 and then professor in 1974.
3. Mary Hesse (1924–2016). She became a lecturer in the history and philosophy of science at Cambridge in 1960 and was professor from 1975 until her retirement in 1985. Her most relevant publication was *Science and the Human Imagination: Aspects of the History and Logic of Physical Science*, London: S.C.M. Press, 1954.
4. Robert Young (1935–2017). From 1964 to 1976 he was a fellow and graduate tutor of King's College and became the first director of the Wellcome Unit for the History of Medicine set up within the Department of History and Philosophy of Science.
5. See F. R. Leavis, *Two Cultures? The Significance of C. P. Snow*, introduction by S. Collini, Cambridge: Cambridge University Press 2013.

field the writings of German theologians such as Bultmann[6] and Tillich.[7] My proposal was to investigate a contemporary philosophical debate by reference to a comparable cross-cultural tension in a particular historical period. The choice of period followed from my earlier explorations – of Coleridge's relations with Thomas Beddoes[8] in connection with 'laughing gas', and of the Cornish society which had produced the young Humphry Davy.[9] The short proposal mentioned several authors whose work had already influenced my thinking – Michael Polanyi,[10] Marjorie Grene,[11] Elizabeth Sewell,[12] Martin Johnson,[13] M. H. Nicolson[14] and Suzanne K. Langer.[15] In retrospect, it is clear that I had no predefined perspective in respect of the relations between literature and science. The texts which I had read represented a confused mixture of perspectives on the question. The intended purpose of the research was to articulate what was thought to be the relationship between 'science' and 'literature' at the end of the eighteenth century. The texts which I had read were arguing both that imagination stimulates scientific advance and that creative writing is informed by new science. My intention was to explore this cross-fertilization in a particular instance.

I held a postgraduate scholarship for three years, from 1966 until 1969. I married in the autumn of 1968 and was given permission to reside in London for the third year of my research. I carried out my research quite independently. I had minimal contact with my director of studies and had no association with the group which, under his leadership, produced the 'May

6. Rudolf Bultmann (1884–1976), particularly *Primitive Christianity in Its Contemporary Setting*, London: Thames and Hudson, 1956.
7. Paul Tillich (1886–1965), particularly *The Courage to Be*, New Haven, CT: Yale University Press, 1952.
8. Thomas Beddoes (1760–1808) was a physician and scientific writer.
9. Humphry Davy (1778–1829) was born in Penzance. In 1798 he became a member of the Pneumatic Institution in Bristol at the instigation of Beddoes. He became a member of the Royal Institution in 1801 and, subsequently, president of the Royal Society in 1820.
10. Michael Polanyi (1891–1976), particularly *Personal Knowledge: Towards a Post-critical Philosophy*, Chicago: University of Chicago Press, 1958.
11. Marjorie Grene (1910–2009), particularly *The Knower and the Known*, New York, Basic Books, 1966.
12. Elizabeth Sewell (1919–2001), particularly *The Orphic Voice: Poetry and Natural History*, New Haven, CT: Yale University Press, 1960.
13. Martin Johnson (1896–1983), particularly *Science and the Meanings of Truth*, London: Faber and Faber, 1946.
14. Marjorie Hope Nicolson (1894–1981), particularly *Newton Demands the Muse*, Princeton, NJ: Princeton University Press, 1946.
15. Suzanne Langer (1895–1985), particularly *Philosophy in a New Key*, New American Library, Mentor Book, 1942.

Day Manifesto'[16] in May 1968 in advance of the General Election of June 1970. I had no involvement with the student revolts in the United Kingdom which reflected the 'May Events' in Paris, in May 1968. As the research developed, it concentrated on the transition in the period from the concern to construct systems of thought unifying science and religion towards an orientation to ground meaning in experience rather than in intellectual commitment. The thesis was submitted in April 1971, and was accepted, after some revision, in 1972.

Priestley (1733–1804) was born to a Dissenting family and educated at a Dissenting Academy. He was a minister to two dissenting congregations before becoming a tutor at the Warrington Dissenting Academy from 1761 until 1767. He was a minister in Leeds from 1767 until 1773, steering his congregation towards Unitarianism. He then moved to Calne to become political advisor to Lord Shelburne (a Unitarian) and tutor to his sons. Shelburne provided him with a laboratory to enable him to pursue his scientific work. In 1780, he moved to become a minister in Birmingham. Priestley was an active supporter of the American and French Revolutions. This provoked local opposition. His congregation's meeting house and his home were destroyed by a mob when he and a few friends were celebrating the second anniversary of the storming of the Bastille in July 1791. He moved to London, teaching and preaching in Hackney. In August 1792, he accepted the French citizenship conferred on him by the French National Assembly. After the declaration of war on France in February 1793, and shortly before Pitt's suspension of Habeas Corpus in May 1794, Priestley sailed to America, living in Pennsylvania until his death in 1804.

Part I of the thesis examined Priestley's attempt to reconcile his theological beliefs with his developing scientific interests. This analysed his publications between 1765 and 1795 which separately considered the nature of political and religious liberty,[17] discussed the relations between natural and revealed religion and between materialism and immaterialism,[18] and offered histories of sciences such as electricity and optics.[19] The analysis explored his efforts to construct a coherently rational system of meaning across intellectual fields, but it suggested that the endeavour was plagued by contradictions and inconsistencies in respect,

---

16. See R. Williams, ed., *The May Day Manifesto 1968*, introduction by O. Jones, New York: Verso Books, 2018.

17. Priestley, *An Essay on the First Principles of Government; and on the Nature of Political, Civil, and Religious Liberty*, Dublin, 1768.

18. Priestley, *Institutes of Natural and Revealed Religion*, 3 vols, London, 1772, and *Disquisitions Relating to Matter and Spirit*, London, 1777.

19. Priestley, *The History and Present State of Electricity with Original Experiments*, London, 1767, and *The History and Present State of Discoveries Relating to Vision, Light, and Colours*, 2 vols, London, 1772.

for instance, of his views whether knowledge – religious and scientific – advances historically or corresponds with unchanging, objective truths, or of his views whether religious conviction is compatible with subservience to state authority.

Priestley was a Unitarian – someone who did not accept the divinity of Christ – and he was a materialist 'necessarian' – a follower of David Hartley's[20] *Observations on Man* (1749) which pursued the logic of Locke's theory of the development of our ideas in a process of association by suggesting that this is a physiologically determined process. We would label Priestley's position as determinist or behaviourist. Born in 1772, Coleridge was the tenth child of a clergyman. By 1794 he had left Cambridge without completing his degree and, with his friend Robert Southey,[21] was planning to establish an ideal society on the banks of the Susquehannah River. He wrote to Southey that he was a 'compleat necessarian'. The project was to establish a 'Pantisocracy' – a community in which all have rule and equal responsibility. The intention was to apply necessarian principles in such a way as to guarantee that initial inno-cence would be sustained by habit to engender an ethical society. While still pursuing this project Coleridge took up various jobs to earn a living – some writing, some lecturing and some preaching (to unitarian congregations). By early 1795, the proposed scheme had collapsed. In part, Coleridge blamed Southey for wanting to take a servant with him to America, in this way showing his total lack of appreciation of Coleridge's guiding philosophy.

Part II of the thesis charted the development of Coleridge's philosoph-ical position away from Hartleian materialism to adherence to views which were a mixture of Neoplatonism and English equivalents of German Nature philosophy. The thesis culminated in an interpretation of Coleridge's *The Ancient Mariner*, written in 1797, as a poem in which the unconsciously deter-mined action of the mariner in shooting the albatross becomes transformed to become the basis of a revelation of the harmony of all created beings in the universe. This interpretation was based on reading the texts which Coleridge himself borrowed from the Bristol public library between 1793 and 1798;[22] analysis of the ways in which he conceptualised his interpersonal relations as exemplifications of a continuous struggle between feeling and reason; discus-sion of the public lectures given in 1795, since categorised as 'Political' and 'Theological' lectures; and his journalistic work of the period.

---

20. David Hartley (1705–1757). Coleridge named his first son as David Hartley Coleridge, born 19 September 1796.
21. Robert Southey (1774–1843) was born in Bristol. He was educated at Westminster School and at Balliol College, Oxford. In August 1794, he and Coleridge collaborated in writing a play – *The Fall of Robespierre* – which was published in October 1794.
22. As disclosed by G. Whalley, 'The Bristol Library Borrowings of Southey and Coleridge, 1795-98', *The Library. Transactions of the Bibliographic Society*, 5th series, 4, 1949, 114–32.

I was constrained by the fact of writing my thesis for the English faculty, causing me to present an interpretation of a poem as the raison d'être of the research. In fact, my primary interest was in the philosophical tensions of the period which led to the emergence of a supposed autonomy of aesthetic expression within which rationally discordant positions might be reconciled. I used recent conceptualisation, such as Horkheimer's distinction between 'subjective' and 'objective' reason[23] as a way of understanding the issues of the historical moment at the end of the eighteenth century, but this did not mean that I adhered to a 'critical theory' position. Rather, I thought my own way through reading the texts of Priestley and Coleridge and their contemporaries. I read, among others, the work of William Godwin,[24] David Hume,[25] Frances Hutcheson,[26] Tom Paine,[27] William Paley,[28] Edmund Burke,[29] William Warburton[30] and William Blackstone.[31] I followed the ideological debate which was largely one between representatives of the Established Church and State and those emanating from dissenting backgrounds and intellectual formation. I examined the English reception of the work of Jean-Jacques Rousseau. This was all work with which Priestley and Coleridge had engaged. Through their engagement I was able to situate schools of thought in relation to different social and institutional positions – particularly the divergent views on reason and feeling associated with Dissenting or Anglican traditions. My chapter on Coleridge's 'Political Lectures' tried to show that Coleridge was not primarily concerned with Pitt's *political* oppression, even though the government's attack on liberty was the specific stimulus for his lectures. Rather, Coleridge was interested in political philosophy as an extension of moral philosophy. The lectures were concerned to have an effect on the political behaviour of his audience. He was hostile to imposed authority and also to the view that behaviour should be regulated by a prescribed moral code and by a sense of obligation to that code. Equally, he was anxious to disown the unregulated actions of Robespierre and his followers, overtly supporting the Girondists rather than

---

23. See Horkheimer, *Eclipse of Reason*, Oxford: Oxford University Press, 1947.
24. Godwin, *An Enquiry Concerning Political Justice, and Its Influence on General Virtue and Happiness*, in two volumes, London, 1793.
25. Hume, *An Enquiry Concerning Human Understanding*, 1748, and *A Treatise of Human Nature*, 1739–40.
26. Hutcheson, *An Enquiry into the Original of Our Ideas of Beauty and Virtue*, 2nd edn, 1726.
27. Paine, *The Age of Reason*, London, 1794.
28. Paley, *The Principles of Moral and Political Philosophy*, 1785.
29. Burke, *A Philosophical Enquiry into the Origin of Our Ideas of the Sublime and Beautiful*, 1757, and *Reflections on the Revolution in France*, 1790.
30. Warburton, *Alliance between Church and State*, 1736
31. Blackstone, *Commentaries on the Laws of England*, 1766.

the Jacobins. He struggled to articulate the view that moral behaviour is naturally self-generated and then reinforced by reasons which proceed to safeguard those feelings, ensuring that they do not become contaminated by actions.

I became eligible to vote for the first time at the General Election of March 1966. This took place about a month before my final examinations and I suspect that I did not vote. In spite of the critique of Harold Wilson made in the May Day Manifesto, I think I would have voted for Labour both in June 1970 and February 1974, on the latter occasion with more conviction as a result of the developments described in the next chapter. During this period, I was immersed in the political philosophy disputes of the late eighteenth century rather than in contemporary practical politics.

B. The Text

As we have seen, the discussion concerning the underlying philosophy of Pantisocracy reached its climax in the autumn and early winter of 1794. The difference between Coleridge and Southey at this time led, first of all, to compromises in the scheme, and, finally, to the breakdown of the friendly relationship between the two poets. During the course of 1795 each became eager to pin the label of apostate on the other. There is no need to attempt to act as judge in this case. Such an appraisal of the situation has no importance for this study. Instead we need to decide what, finally, was the influence of Southey's thought and behaviour on the personality of Coleridge, or, more significantly, on the way Coleridge viewed his own personality and conceived the nature of personality abstractly. We also need to look at the way in which Coleridge set about the task of adapting the ideas which he had formulated for the creation of a 'new' society to the ordinary society which he and Southey chose to call 'morbid'.[32] The answers to these questions are most clearly found in the *Political Lectures* which Coleridge delivered in the early part of 1795.

Coleridge delivered three political lectures in the period between late January and early March, 1795. The first was published late in February under the title *A Moral and Political Lecture*, and it was revised and republished in November as the *Introductory Address* to *Conciones ad Populum*. This latter publication contained a lecture entitled *On the Present War* which consisted of the second and possibly parts of the third lecture that had been delivered in February. Coleridge's 'third' political lecture of 1795 which was, therefore, in fact, the fourth, was delivered as a *Lecture on the Two Bills* on 26 November

---

32. For Southey's realisation that Godwin's theories were utopian, see a letter to Grosvenor Bedford of 1 October 1795, in C. C. Southey, *The Life and Correspondence*, vol. 1, 247.

1795, and published as *The Plot Discovered*, after revision and expansion, in the same month.[33]

Although *The Plot Discovered* was the last lecture to be 'delivered', it provides the most useful introduction to the nature and scope of Coleridge's thinking in the whole group. It was 'delivered' against ministerial treason. Habeas Corpus had been suspended on 17 May 1794, and state trials for treason were held between October and December of that year. Tooke,[34] Hardy[35] and Thelwall[36] were acquitted, but the government continued to encroach upon the liberty of the people. Government attempts to limit the liberty of the press and freedom of speech constituted the real treason in Coleridge's view. The Treason and Convention Bills were introduced on November 6 and 10, respectively, by Lord Grenville and William Pitt, and were put into effect on December 18. At the time of Coleridge's lecture, the Treason Bill had passed its third reading in the Lords and its second in the Commons, and the Convention Bill had passed its first reading in the Commons and had not yet been introduced into the Lords.[37]

The most immediately striking feature of *The Plot Discovered* is the similarity of many of the attitudes to the orthodox line of rational dissent of which Coleridge would have been particularly aware from the speeches of William Frend which he had heard as an undergraduate. The rational position with its specific connotations as manifested in Unitarianism is evident in the following opening passage:

'THE MASS OF THE PEOPLE HAVE NOTHING TO DO WITH THE LAWS, BUT TO OBEY THEM!' – Ere yet this foul treason against the majesty of man, ere yet this blasphemy against the goodness of God be registered among our statutes, I enter my protest! Ere yet our laws as well as our religion be muffled up in mysteries, as a CHRISTIAN I protest against this worse than Pagan darkness![38]

---

33. (See Lewis Patton and Peter Mann, eds, 1971, *The Collected Works of Samuel Taylor Coleridge, Vol. 1: Lectures 1795 On Politics and Religion*, London: Routledge & Kegan Paul, 1971, xxv–xxxiii). I use the *Introductory Address* as my source for what, throughout, I call *A Moral and Political Lecture*, and I use *The Plot Discovered* as my source for the lecture which was delivered as a *Lecture on the Two Bills*. [...]

34. John Horne Tooke (1736–1812).

35. Thomas Hardy (1752–1832) – 'radical politician', *Dictionary of National Biography*, Vol. 24, 357–58.

36. John Thelwall (1764–1834).

37. For a general survey of the political atmosphere of the 1790s, see J. H. Plumb, *England in the Eighteenth Century (1714-1815)*, Part III. 'The Age of Pitt', London: Pelican, 1960. Also see C. Hobhouse, *Fox*, London: Constable, 1934.

38. Coleridge, *The Plot Discovered* (Patton and Mann, *Lectures 1795*, 285).

In objecting to the idea of obedience to laws with which people have nothing to do, Coleridge is rebelling against the notion of objectivity. This form of mindless obedience that is required is treason against the majesty of man because it scorns his reason, and it is blasphemy against God because He endowed man with reason above the beasts. Coleridge objects to 'mysteries' because both law and religion must be rationally explicable. Elaborating his position, Coleridge continues:

> In all ministerial measures there are two reasons, the real, and the ostensible. The ostensible reason of the present Bill we have heard; the real reason will not elude the search of common sagacity. The existing laws of Treason were too clear, too unequivocal. Judges indeed (what will not Judges do?) Judges might endeavour to transfer to these laws their own flexibility; Judges might make strange interpretations. But English Juries could not, would not understand them. Hence instead of eight hecatombs of condemned traitors behold eight triumphant acquitted felons! Hinc illae lacrymae. – The present Bills were conceived and laid in the dunghill of despotism among the other yet unhatched eggs of the old Serpent. In due time and in fit opportunity they crawled into light. Genius of Britain! Crush them![39]

The new measures were really taken to obscure the existing laws of treason. Implicit in Coleridge's attitude, therefore, is the feeling that law must be as clear and universally known as possible. In this, Coleridge is like Frend. Paley had advocated flexibility and expediency, but Coleridge is hostile to this position because he identifies expediency with malice on the part of the government.[40] Like Frend again, Coleridge here expresses belief in juries, not in judges, and he regards the recent trials as the vindication of the jury system. The following words could be Frend's:

> But I hear it suggested, that the two Acts will not be administered in all their possible stretch of implication! Pale-hearted men, who cannot approve, yet who dare not oppose a most foul ministry, is it come to this, that Britons should depend on clemency not justice, that Britons should whine to Ministers to stand between them and the law?[41]

---

39. Coleridge, *The Plot Discovered* (Patton and Mann, *Lectures 1795*, 288).
40. For Paley's attitude, see *The Principles of Moral and Political Philosophy* (1785), Bk. VI, Section VIII: Of the administration of justice, in *The Works of William Paley*, vol. 4, London, 1825, 419.
41. Coleridge, *The Plot Discovered* (Patton and Mann, *Lectures 1795*, 291).

This is the rigid legalism that Frend had represented in opposition to Milner in Coleridge's days as an undergraduate.

Nevertheless, this lecture also contains Coleridge's typical insistence on the primacy of feeling. Coleridge argues that, in origin, Majesty meant the unity of the people, the weight imparted by the majority. The ancient Lex Majestatis or Law of Treason was intended against those who injured the People. It is in this context that he claims that the feelings of the people are sacred, and that the bills now under consideration prohibit the expression of these feelings. Coleridge says:

> The Bill now pending is indeed as full-foliaged, as the Manchineel tree; (and like the manchineel, will poison those who are fools enough to slumber beneath it) but its import is briefly this – first, that the people of England should possess no unrestrained right of consulting in common on common grievances: and secondly, that Mr. Thelwall should no longer give political lectures.[42]

Coleridge develops this reference to Thelwall. His main argument is that the voice of an individual is suppressed by a government which is aware that it is the voice of the whole people and not just of an individual. In making this point, Coleridge makes explicit several assumptions concerning true and false feelings. He remarks:

> The public amusements at the Theatre are already under ministerial control. And if the tremendous sublimity of Schiller, if 'the Robbers' can be legally suppressed by that thing yclept a Lord Chamberlain, in point of literary exhibition it would be unreasonable for Mr. Thelwall to complain. But in proportion as he feels himself of little consequence he will perceive the situation of the ministry is desperate. Nothing could make him of importance but that he speaks the feelings of multitudes. The feelings of men are always founded in truth. The modes of expressing them may be blended with error, and the feelings themselves may lead to the most abhorred excess. Yet still they are originally right: they teach man that something is wanting, something which he ought to have. Now if the premier with the influence of the wealthy and the prejudice of the ignorant on his side, were evidently struggling to supply these perceived desiderata, could an unsupported malcontent oppose him? Alas! It is the vice of this nation, that if a minister merely promise to increase the comforts or enlarge the liberties of the people, he instantly conjures

---

42. Coleridge, *The Plot Discovered* (Patton and Mann, *Lectures 1795*, 296).

up such a wild and overwhelming popularity, as enables him to execute with impunity the most ruinous schemes against both. But William Pitt knows, that Thelwall is the voice of tens of thousands, and he levels his parliamentary thunder-bolts against him with the same emotion with which Caligula wished to see the whole Roman state brought together in one neck, that he might have the luxury of beheading it at *one* moment. But we shall revert to this clause in due time, and gird ourselves up to this consideration of the restrictions of the right of petitioning.[43]

In the few sentences discussing feeling, Coleridge begins to grapple with the problem which is to concern him most when he later enters into correspondence with Thelwall. Coleridge had always assumed that correct feelings would necessarily manifest themselves in correct behaviour, and that, therefore, to assess the behaviour of a person was the same thing as to assess the feelings of that person. The problem was that Hartleian association tried to combine this theory of an internal necessity of expression with the theory that expression and external impression also necessarily affected the personality. With regard to expression, the Hartleian position was circular since if there was an internal necessity of association of which expression was the end product, that product could hardly corrupt the process of which it was itself the culmination.

With regard to external impression, the Hartleian position tended to overlook the continuity of such impressions. Hartley tended to postulate two significant static moments, the first of which was the moment when the mind initially received associations from external impression, and the second of which was the moment when the mind reached a stage of final perfection after a process of internal amelioration developing from those initial impressions. No allowance was made for interplay between inner and outer.[44] Coleridge had held both aspects of the Hartleian view and was confronted by the problem that I have detailed. He had always wanted to insist that external impressions modified internal feelings, but he had hardly reconciled this view with his belief in an inner necessity. The progress of the French Revolution seemed

---

43. Coleridge, *The Plot Discovered* (Patton and Mann, *Lectures 1795*, 296–97).
44. See the following passage from Hartley's *Observations on Man*, Part II, Proposition 69, p. 291:

> For though our Affections are not directly and immediately subject to the voluntary power, yet our Actions are; *and consequently our Affections* also mediately. He that at first practises Acts of Benevolence by Constraint, and continues to practise them, will at last have associated such a Variety of Pleasures with them, as to transfer a great instantaneous Pleasure upon them and beget in himself the Affections *from which they naturally flow.* In like manner, if we abstain from malevolent Actions, we shall dry up the ill Passions, which are their Sources. (italics added)

to illustrate clearly that correct feelings could be corrupted disastrously. Was Coleridge to conclude that there can be disparity between an original feeling and its expression, or was he to retain a belief in necessity which would lead him to deduce that the atrocities of the French Revolution proved the falsity of its underlying feelings? The passage cited above shows that he chose the former course, that his tenacious grip on necessity loosened slightly. He accepts that 'modes of expressing' feelings may be in error, and that the feelings themselves, although pure and truthful 'may lead to the most abhorred excesses'. The solution that Coleridge finds here has a Miltonic ring, as do many of the sentiments expressed in the lectures. Miltonic Platonism was the main concrete source for the kind of Shaftesburyanism that began to transform Coleridge's Rousseauistic leanings and to plug the hole that experience of personal and political realities had made in Hartleian necessarianism.[45] Feelings still do not have the status of innate ideas, but Coleridge uses the idea of ignorance and error to explain the corruption of pure feeling. Rational misunderstanding corrupts purity of heart. But if correct generalised feelings are learnt and are the particular human feelings directed to a different, rationally ascertained context, how can one be sure that this first rational direction is not a misunderstanding of the general situation? If Coleridge is to retain his belief in learnt feelings and the possible manipulation of feelings, he must now be prepared to accept that these original feelings may be mislearnt and falsely manipulated. By accepting that reason can destroy the purity of feeling, Coleridge must assert the purity of feeling before experience and before reason if he is to remain an optimist, and if he is to accept the a priori goodness of feeling he must accept human feelings as they are, in their particular, natural context before their manipulation for the purposes of a rationally considered social

---

45. Milton was certainly not the only origin of the change in Coleridge's thinking in 1795, but this is not the place to develop arguments for other possible influences. Coleridge's reading of Akenside may have familiarised him with Leibniz, and his reading of Cudworth must also have presented the case of the Platonic tradition in England. For Coleridge's reading at this time, see G. Whalley, 'The Bristol Library Borrowings of Southey and Coleridge, 1793-8', *The Library. Transactions of the Bibliographic Society*, 5th Series, 4, 1949, 114–32; See R. Cudworth, *The True Intellectual System of the Universe*, 2nd ed., 2 vols., London: Bloomsbury, 1743; and J. A. Passmore, *Ralph Cudworth. An Interpretation*, Cambridge: Cambridge University Press, 1951; C. E, Lowrey, *The Philosophy of Ralph Cudworth*, New York, 1884; Paul Janet, *Essai sur le médiateur plastique de Cudworth*, Paris, 1860.

See M. Akenside, *The Pleasures of Imagination. A Poem in Three Books*, London, 1744; R. W. Chapman, 'A Note on the First Edition of *The Pleasures of Imagination*', *Review of English Studies*, I, 1925, 346–48; J. Hart, 'Akenside's Revision of *The Pleasures of Imagination*', *Proceedings of the Modern Languages Association of America*, 74, 1959, 67–74; G. R. Potter, 'Mark Akenside, Prophet of Evolution', *Modern Philology*, 24, 1926, 55–64; W. L. Renwick, 'Akenside and Others', *Durham University Journal*, 1942, 34.

utility. Paradoxically, the rejection of Hartley's kind of necessarian position involves the rejection of the possibility of transforming humans and human society.

Not only does Coleridge accept the disjunction of feeling and behaviour, but the discussion of sedition also causes him to recognise that the truth of feeling is prior to verbal expression and is often distorted by it. Coleridge says in this context:

> Our ancestors were wisely cautious in framing the bill of treason; they would not admit words as sufficient evidence of intention. How often does the tongue utter what the moment after the heart disapproves! These indiscretions are blameable in the individual, but the frequency of them was honourable to the nation at large, as it demonstrated the unsuspecting sprit of a free government, too proud to be jealous![46]

[...]

In this passage there is the sense that the real human motivations are sub-verbal and that a good government should allow for the interplay of persons rather than conduct affairs on the basis of the interplay of words. The immediate effect of Coleridge's acceptance that feeling could be totally corrupted by erroneous reason was to ensure that correct reasons were inculcated rather than to investigate the nature of the feeling which was before experience. Coleridge had underrated reason when it was opposed to feeling as a rival determinant of the nature of a person, but as Coleridge's view of feeling gradually became equated with his conception of being itself, so he became prepared to accept the subsidiary modifying influence of reason, and to see that if the feeling self is beyond or before experience then the only way to alter persons is to influence reason's subsidiary role. Hence Coleridge's combination of a strong belief in both feeling and reason in his *Political Lectures*.

The introduction to *A Moral and Political Lecture* begins with an analysis of the audience of the lecture and also of the present state of the French Revolution. In this analysis Coleridge uses phrases which are sometimes reminiscent of Southey. The important point is that Coleridge now systematically accepts the need for 'fixed principles' to modify the force of the feeling self, whereas Southey had tried to make rationality the essence of being. Coleridge begins the lecture which he delivered first of the three in the following manner:

> Companies resembling the present will, from a variety of circumstances, consist *chiefly* of the zealous Advocates for Freedom. It will therefore

---

46. Coleridge, *The Plot Discovered* (Patton and Mann, *Lectures 1795*, 291).

be our endeavour, not so much to excite the torpid, as to regulate the feelings of the ardent: and above all, to evince the necessity of *bottoming* on fixed Principles, that so we may not be the unstable Patriots of Passion or Accident, nor hurried away by names of which we have not sifted the meaning, and by tenets of which we have not examined the consequences. The Times are trying; and in order to be prepared against their difficulties, we should have acquired a prompt facility of adverting in all our doubts to some grand and comprehensive Truth. In a deep and strong Soil must that Tree fix its Roots, the height of which is to 'reach to Heaven, and the Sight of it to the ends of all the Earth'.

The Example of France is indeed a 'Warning to Britain'. A Nation wading to their Rights through Blood, and marking the track of Freedom by Devastation! Yet let us not embattle our Feelings against our Reason. Let us not indulge our malignant Passions under the mask of Humanity. Instead of railing with infuriate declamation against these excesses, we shall be more profitably employed in developing the sources of them. French Freedom is the Beacon, which while it guides to Equality, should shew us the Dangers that throng the road.[47]

Coleridge is making a plea for rationality and sanity in highly emotional times. He has recourse to the form of an objective criterion in that he argues that actions should be assessed in the light of a 'comprehensive Truth'. This form, in fact, embraces the product of Coleridge's thinking concerning the supremacy of feeling, for the 'comprehensive Truth' to which Coleridge refers without elaboration, must, by implication, involve the principle that person-to-person relationships are of prime importance before all verbal rationalisations. This understanding of Coleridge's assumption is able to make sense of the second paragraph of his lecture. The original feelings which were the foundations of the French impetus for freedom should not be rejected because our feelings are outraged by the atrocities in France. Our reason must channel our feeling so that we accept that French feeling went astray because it was not controlled by reason. If our feelings in reaction are not controlled as the original French feelings should have been, then our reaction is in danger of being as atrocious as are the manifestations of French lack of control. It would not matter that our feelings could react under 'the mask of Humanity'; indeed, French feeling went sour under the same mask. The criterion which must be consulted is not the kind of abstraction, like 'Humanity', which becomes detached from feeling, but the grand belief in feeling itself as a 'comprehensive Truth',

---

47. Coleridge, *Conciones ad Populum* (Patton and Mann, *Lectures 1795*, 33–34).

the belief in a sub-verbal form of human empathy. Coleridge's hatred of abstractions is not unlike Burke's,[48] but he would differ radically from Burke because he would argue that, mistakenly, Burke had rejected the 'thing' as well as the 'name' of freedom. French Freedom had taken a wrong turning and had become systematised and inhuman, but this did not mean that true human relationships in freedom were impossible. French freedom had become corrupted because the abstraction had become the belief of an intelligent elite, whilst there had been no attempt to foster the practice of 'openness' by sharing freedom through a process of democratisation. Coleridge makes this point in his next paragraph:

> The Annals of the French Revolution have recorded in Letters of Blood, that the Knowledge of the Few cannot counteract the Ignorance of the Many; that the Light of Philosophy, when it is confined to a small Minority, points out the Possessors as the Victims, rather than the Illuminators, of the Multitude. The Patriots of France either hastened into the dangerous and gigantic Error of making certain Evil the means of contingent Good, or were sacrificed by the Mob, with whose prejudices and ferocity their unbending Virtue forbade them to assimilate.[49]

Coleridge proceeds to examine the dilemma of some of the French leaders. His comments on the Girondists are interesting because, certainly viewing from a later date, they might also seem to be self-regarding:

> Men of genius are rarely either prompt in action or consistent in general conduct: their early habits have been those of contemplative indolence; and the day-dreams, with which they have been accustomed to amuse their solitude, adapt them for splendid speculation, not temperate and practicable counsels.[50]

The phrase Coleridge uses to describe Brissot[51] – 'a sublime visionary'[52] – forces the likeness home, but clearly at the time of speaking Coleridge wishes to hold

48. For Burke, *Reflections on the Revolution in France*, introduction by A. J. Grieve, London, Dent, 1964; C. Parkin, *The Moral Basis of Burke's Political Thought*, New York: Russell and Russell, 1956; A. Cobban, *Edmund Burke and the Revolt against the Eighteenth Century*, London: Allen and Unwin, 1929.
49. Coleridge, *Conciones ad Populum* (Patton and Mann, *Lectures 1795*, 34).
50. Coleridge, *Conciones ad Populum* (Patton and Mann, *Lectures 1795*, 34).
51. Jean-Pierre Brissot (1754–1793). *Biographie Universelle*, vol. 5, 568–70.
52. Coleridge, *Conciones ad Populum* (Patton and Mann, *Lectures 1795*, 35).

such speculators in contempt. His main objection to Robespierre is that his idealism became abstracted from practical possibility:

> I rather think, that the distant prospect, to which he was travelling, appeared to him grand and beautiful; but that he fixed his eye on it with such intense eagerness as to neglect the foulness of the road. If however his first intentions were pure, his subsequent enormities yield us a melancholy proof, that it is not the character of the possessor which directs the power, but the power which shapes and depraves the character of the possessor. In Robespierre, its influence was assisted by the properties of his disposition. – Enthusiasm, even in the gentlest temper, will frequently generate sensations of an unkindly order. If we clearly perceive any one thing to be of vast and infinite importance to ourselves and all mankind, our first feelings impel us to turn with angry contempt from those, who doubt and oppose it. The ardour of undisciplined benevolence seduces us into malignity: and whenever our hearts are warm, and our objects great and excellent, intolerance is the sin that does most easily beset us. But this enthusiasm in Robespierre was blended with gloom, and suspiciousness, and inordinate vanity.[53]

Coleridge himself had become an enthusiast of Pantisocracy to such an extent that he had become intolerant of Southey's warmth of feeling for his family. Later in the lecture Coleridge does not let Southey's type of apostasy escape unmentioned,[54] but his comments here illustrate his own newly moderated attitude. Love and tolerance are the keynotes of this lecture, and an emphasis on acceptance of persons regardless of their sentiments or their behaviour, both of which are superficial adjuncts to the real self. Coleridge's lectures themselves are evidence of a practical desire to communicate, and this desire is sustained later in the publication of *The Watchman*.

---

53. Coleridge, *Conciones ad Populum* (Patton and Mann, *Lectures 1795*, 35).
54. See Coleridge, *Conciones ad Populum* (Patton and Mann, *Lectures 1795*, 40), and also *Conciones ad Populum* (Patton and Mann, *Lectures 1795*, 48). This last passage runs:

    All that can delight the poor man's senses or strengthen his understanding, you preclude; yet with generous condescension you would bid him exclaim 'LIBERTY and EQUALITY!' because, forsooth, he should possess the same Right to an Hovel which you claim to a Palace.

    In a note, Patton and Mann suggest that this may be directed against Burke, but it is possible that an attack nearer to home is intended if the similarity between the argument employed here and that used against Southey in Griggs (E. L. Griggs, *Coleridge Collected Letters*, vol. 1, letter 65, Oxford: Clarendon Press, 1956, 114) is noted. Hence Coleridge had used this argument against Southey as early as October, 1794.

In the analysis of kinds of Democrats which follows the account of the progress of the French Revolution, Coleridge begins by condemning the fact that both theology and 'political ideology are judged as abstractions without reference to persons. The limited ground that is shared with Burke is again apparent:

> The majority of Democrats appear to me to have attained that portion of knowledge in politics, which infidels possess in religion. I would by no means be supposed to imply, that the objections of both are equally unfounded, but that they both attribute to the system which they reject, all the evils existing under it; and that both contemplating truth and justice 'in the nakedness of abstraction', condemn constitutions and dispensations without having sufficiently examined the natures, circumstances, and capacities of their recipients.[55]

Coleridge distinguishes three kinds of false Democrat. The first class comprises those whose opinions depend entirely on the reports of what is happening in France, and who therefore oscillate without fixed principles. The second class comprises militant enthusiasts. The idea of force gains popularity in unenlightened minds and amongst those who are underprivileged. Coleridge accepts that these people are beyond the reach of rational persuasion. In the following passage, tolerance figures as the ideal and Coleridge begins to realise that in some circumstances this ideal can only be communicated by subsidiary feelings rather than subsidiary reason. Feelings must now come to the aid of the insistence on personhood which had been derived from them. In other words, Coleridge still has insufficient faith in the ability of the true feeling self to assert itself so that when rational control is inapplicable, indirect control by feeling must be exerted from without. This is a retreat to a Rousseauistic position as manifested in 'Émile'.[56] Coleridge says:

> The purifying alchemy of Education may transmute the fierceness of an ignorant man into virtuous energy – but what remedy shall we apply to him, whom Plenty has not softened, whom Knowledge has not taught Benevolence? This is one among the many fatal effects which result from the want of fixed principles. Convinced that vice is error, we shall entertain sentiments of Pity for the vicious, not of Indignation – and even with respect to that bad Man, to whom we have before alluded, altho' we are now groaning beneath the burden of his misconduct, we shall

---

55. Coleridge, *Conciones ad Populum* (Patton and Mann, *Lectures 1795*, 37).
56. See J. -J. Rousseau. *Émile, ou de l'éducation.*

harbour no sentiments of Revenge; but rather *condole* with him that his chaotic Iniquities have exhibited such a complication of extravagance, inconsistency, and rashness as may *alarm* him with apprehensions of approaching lunacy![57]

We shall see shortly that Coleridge develops practical plans for the communication of his ideal to the underprivileged, but implicit in the first sentence of the above passage is the inherent danger of the retreat to which I have drawn attention, that the new ideal of person-to-person relationship and tolerance has to be taught as much as 'the mask of Humanity' and is as detached from persons and practicality. This becomes clear when, after distinguishing the third class of Democrat as comprising those who want to be equal with those above them in status but want to keep the poor underneath – a category into which, perhaps, Southey was seen to fall – Coleridge then describes the characteristics of the true Democrat. Coleridge's enthusiasm runs away with him and he falls into the trap that he had earlier exposed:

We turn with pleasure to the contemplation of that small but glorious band, whom we may truly distinguish by the name of thinking and disinterested Patriots. These are the men who have encouraged the sympathetic passions till they have become irresistible habits, and made their duty a necessary part of their self-interest, by the long continued cultivation of that moral taste which derives our most exquisite pleasures from the contemplation of possible perfection, and proportionate pain from the perception of existing *depravation*. Accustomed to regard all the affairs of man as a process, they never hurry and they never pause. Theirs is not that twilight of political knowledge which gives us just light enough to place one foot before the other; as they advance the scene still opens upon them, and they press right onward with a vast and various landscape of existence around them. Calmness and energy mark all their actions. Convinced that vice originates not in the man, but in the surrounding circumstances; not in the heart, but in the understanding; he is hopeless concerning no one – to correct as vice or generate a virtuous conduct he pollutes not his hands with the scourge of coercion; but by endeavouring to alter the circumstances would remove, or by strengthening the intellect, disarms, the temptation.[58]

---

57. Coleridge, *Conciones ad Populum*, 18 (Patton and Mann, *Lectures 1795*, 39).
58. Coleridge, *Conciones ad Populum* (Patton and Mann, *Lectures 1795*, 40).

Two major points of interest emerge from this passage. The first I have already suggested and that is that in describing the characteristics of the true Democrats, Coleridge isolates for praise a group of people that constitutes an elite and a state of mind that can only be called 'visionary'. The detachment and impracticality that Coleridge had attacked in Brissot and the Girondists are favourably attached to the true Democrat, so much so that Coleridge can take delight in the prospect of soaring 'above the present state of humanity'. However, we are faced here with a seeming inconsistency only because we have not understood that the 'visionary' aspect of the true Democrat is seen by Coleridge as only one aspect, and this is the second point of major interest. The key to the distinctive feature of the true Democrat as envisaged by Coleridge is the following sentence: 'Calmness and energy mark all their actions'. Energy is gradually taken by Coleridge, especially through contact with Thelwall, to be synonymous with 'being'. Also through contact with Thelwall, this concept of being comes into contact with physiological theory through such related designations as 'vital energy', 'animal vitality' and 'animal magnetism'. The question which is now to concern Coleridge most forcibly, both abstractly and personally, is how, on the one hand, the calm contemplation of right ends can be indulged without the loss of energy, and, on the other, how energetic activity can be achieved without losing the consciousness of its aims and purposes. To put the matter personally, Coleridge wanted to be a speculator and an activist. He idealised the conjunction of the two in his picture of the true Democrat, but much of his thinking from this point onwards revolves around the fear that the two may be mutually exclusive.

Coleridge returns to the problem of communication. He comments:

> The Author of an essay on political Justice considers private Societies as the sphere of real utility – that (each one illuminating those immediately beneath him), Truth by a gradual descent may at last reach the lowest order. But this is rather plausible than just or practicable. Society as at present constituted does not resemble a chain that ascends in a continuity of Links.[59]

Godwin's solution is not satisfactory,[60] and Coleridge goes on to claim that the best method of communication is to go among the poor like the Methodists.[61]

---

59. Coleridge, *Conciones ad Populum* (Patton and Mann, *Lectures 1795*, 43).
60. See W. Godwin, *An Enquiry Concerning Political Justice, and Its Influence on General Virtue and Happiness*, London, 1795, Bk. IV. Chapter II. Section III. Of Political Associations, 205–19, for the discussion of this issue.
61. See Coleridge, *Conciones ad Populum* (Patton and Mann, *Lectures 1795*, 43).

Religion is the most efficient way of communicating a sense of duty to the lower classes. In an ideal world, domestic affection would stimulate correct attitudes, but, in reality, many family responsibilities are so burdensome amongst the poor that true feelings become distorted and can only be resurrected by reference to a future ideal beyond ordinary experience. The language of the following passage is Paleyan, which indicates that Coleridge is hovering on the brink of contradiction:

> Domestic affections depend on association. We love an object if, as often as we see or recollect it, an agreeable sensation arises in our minds. But alas! How should *he* glow with the charities of Father and Husband, who gaining scarcely more than his own necessities demand, must have been accustomed to regard his wife and children, not as the Soothers of finished labour, but as rivals for the insufficient meal! In a man so circumstanced the Tyranny of the *Present* can be overpowered only by the tenfold mightiness of the *Future*. Religion will cheer his gloom with her promises, and by habituating his mind to anticipate an infinitely great Revolution hereafter, may prepare it even for the sudden reception of a less degree of amelioration in this World.[62]

Coleridge is unhappy with the situation of the poor family, but he places greater faith than before in the potentiality for goodness of the healthy family. He now regards undervaluation of the family as the first step away from particular, personal feeling towards the abyss of abstraction. In the following passage in which Coleridge is moving towards the concluding advice of his lecture, he tries to tie up some of the loose threads of his thoughts. He insists that fixed principles are necessary, but he is anxious to argue that these principles must be the precursors of action and not static conceptions acting as detached arbiters of behaviour. Indeed, principles should not even be the precursors of action but should be participants in it undergoing constant reformulation. Coleridge is concerned to avoid a duality of calmness against energy, wisdom against ardour. Action consolidates the principles which underlie further action. Even mistaken action is better than no action at all, since a mistake may lead to active wisdom whereas a position which eschews action will be valueless even if it is wise. For Coleridge, a lack of concern for immediate family through a concern for general benevolence is indicative of a stagnant wisdom that has become cut off from the roots of human feeling. Coleridge proclaims:

---

62. Coleridge, *Conciones ad Populum* (Patton and Mann, *Lectures 1795*, 45).

But if we hope to instruct others, we should familiarise our own minds to some fixed and determinate principles of action. The World is a vast labyrinth, in which almost every one is running a different way, and almost every one manifesting hatred to those who do not run the same way. A few indeed stand motionless, and not seeking to lead themselves or others out of the maze laugh at the failure of their brethren. Yet with little reason: for more grossly than the most bewildered wanderer does *he* err, who never aims to go right. It is more honourable to the Head, as well as the Heart, to be misled by our eagerness in the pursuit of Truth, than to be safe from blundering by contempt of it. The happiness of Mankind is the *end* of Virtue, and Truth is the Knowledge of the *means*; which he will never seriously attempt to discover, who has not habitually interested himself in the welfare of others. The searcher after Truth must love and be beloved; for general Benevolence is a necessary motive to constancy of pursuit; and this general Benevolence is begotten and rendered permanent by social and domestic affections. Let us beware of that proud Philosophy, which affects to inculcate Philanthropy while it denounces every home-born feeling, by which it is produced and nurtured. The paternal and filial duties discipline the Heart and prepare it for the love of all Mankind. The intensity of private attachments encourages, not prevents, universal Benevolence. The nearer we approach to the Sun, the more intense his heat: yet what corner of the system does not cheer and vivify?[63]

Some of the complexity of Coleridge's position can be gathered from the difference of emphasis between two of his final exhortations. Towards the end of the lecture he says:

The Man who would find Truth, must likewise seek it with an humble and simple Heart, otherwise he will be precipitant and overlook it; or he will be prejudiced, and refuse to see it. *To emancipate itself from the Tyranny of Association*, is the most arduous effort of the mind, particularly in Religious and Political disquisitions. The asserter of the system has associated with it the preservation of Order and public Virtue; the oppugner Imposture, and Wars, and Rapine. Hence, when they dispute, each trembles at the consequences of the other's opinions instead of attending to his train of arguments. Of this however we may be certain, whether we be Christians or Infidels, Aristocrats or Republicans, that our minds are in a state unsusceptible of Knowledge, when we feel an

---

63. Coleridge, *Conciones ad Populum* (Patton and Mann, *Lectures 1795*, 45–46).

eagerness to detect the Falsehood of an Adversary's reasonings, not a sincere wish to discover if there be Truth in them; – when we examine an argument in order that we may answer it, instead of answering because we have examined it.[64]

Here Coleridge is drawing attention to the difficulty of having a tolerant, feeling-ful relationship with other people on account of the distorting and distancing effect of rationally held opinions. It is this emphasis on the purity of being before words and before behaviour that seems to be the basis for the developments in Coleridge's thinking which take him beyond the defence of toleration. By contrast, the final words of the lecture seem to advocate the new emphasis by recourse to old terminology. Coleridge says:

> For this 'subdued sobriety' of temper a practical faith in the doctrine of philosophical necessity seems the only preparative. That vice is the effect of error and the offspring of surrounding circumstances, the object there-fore of condolence not of anger, is a proposition easily understood, and as easily demonstrated. But to make it spread from the understanding to the affections, to call it into action, not only in the great exertions of Patriotism, but in the daily and hourly occurrences of social life, requires the most watchful attentions of the most energetic mind. It is not enough that we have once swallowed these Truths – we must feed on them, as insects on a leaf, till the whole heart be coloured by their qualities, and shew its food in every the minutest fibre.
>
> Finally, in the words of an Apostle, Watch ye! Stand fast in the principles of which ye have been convinced! Quit yourselves like Men! Be strong! Yet let all things be done in the spirit of Love.[65]

Coleridge again shows his anxiety that principles should be applied. The quotation from the Apostle shows Coleridge's concern for the conjunction of feeling and principle in action. However, he here retains aspects of the necessarian view which justify tolerance on the grounds that all men are externally determined, whereas we have seen that Coleridge was really grappling with tolerance as a positive expression of the relations of persons

---

64. Coleridge, *Conciones ad Populum* (Patton and Mann, *Lectures 1795*, 47).
65. Coleridge, *Concuiones ad Populum* (Patton and Mann, *Lectures 1795*, 49).

to persons. It is interesting that Coleridge uses an organic image[66] to describe the process of transformation that he had originally held, from principle to confirmed feeling, at the time when he was on the verge of recognising feeling itself, not as a faculty of being, but somehow as the organic essence of being.

---

66. Coleridge uses the same image in a letter written at the height of his Pantisocratic thinking in October 1794 (see Griggs, *Coleridge Collected Letters*, vol. 1, letter 65, 1956, 115). This supports my feeling that the final passage of the lecture covers up new insights with old language.

Chapter 3

REFLECTIONS ON CITIZENSHIP AND NATIONHOOD FROM BRUBAKER'S ACCOUNT ON FRANCE AND GERMANY [1993]

A. The Background

It did not occur to me at all at the time that I was researching for my PhD that there was a coincidence between my life course and that of Coleridge. I was 22 years old when I began my research, as was Coleridge when he gave his first political lecture. He was already married and was trying various ways to earn a living. My state scholarship ended after three years and I too was then looking for employment. Working in the Civil Service, my wife was our breadwinner. I taught courses for the Workers' Education Association and for the University of London Department of Extra-Mural Studies while applying for university teaching posts. I assumed that my doctoral research was a preparation for an 'academic' career. Although Coleridge and Wordsworth had, famously, been under surveillance of a government agent in the Quantocks, Coleridge was not an activist. He related to an *idea* of politics, to notions of individual liberty and citizenship, rather than to the cut and thrust of political behaviour. He opposed Pitt's suppression of liberty, but he does not appear to have been interested in the debates within parliament between, for instance, Pitt and Fox. Of course, the 'people' whom he addressed in his lectures were not necessarily electors since the suffrage was limited, and there was no sense in which he was involved in swaying the opinions of the MPs who 'represented' his audience in parliament. His support for his friend John Thelwall,[1] who was tried for treason in 1794,[2] was a form of vicarious activism. As he put it in later life, he existed 'collaterally' – a position which became institutionalised

---

1. John Thelwall (1764–1834). He helped to establish the London Corresponding Society in 1792.
2. He spent time in the Tower and in Newgate before he was acquitted.

in his belief in the need for a 'clerisy' within society which would substitute for the Established Church in disseminating values. I was conscious that I was exploring, through my research into the development of Coleridge's thinking from adherence to a system of materialist Unitarianism towards a moralistic Rousseauism, my own transition from nonconformist conviction to a form of existential religious commitment. In this respect my research was instrumental in encouraging substantive changes in my thinking, but this was all taking place in a context which institutionally continued to objectify the detachment which was indirectly the consequence of the supposed legacy of 'late' Coleridge. (His *On the Constitution of the Church and State, According to the idea of Each* of 1830 influenced Newman's *The Idea of a University*, 1858, and 'late' Coleridge was philosophically appropriated by the Oxford idealist tradition[3]). The *form* of the context within which I did my research, that of the liberal university, was an embodiment of the position which was emerging in Coleridge's thought during the late 1790s. The work of Priestley, Paine and Godwin was all the product of the alternative, dissenting tradition which became marginalised in the nineteenth century.

My search for an academic post ended in the autumn of 1969 when I was appointed a lecturer in English literature in Barking Regional College of Technology, which was soon, in January 1970, to become one of the con-stituent colleges of the newly instituted North-East London Polytechnic (NELP). This quickly became known as one of the most radical of the new institutions partly because its deputy director – Eric Robinson, who had been a special advisor to Anthony Crosland in developing the 'binary divide' in British HE – had already published *The New Polytechnics. The People's Universities* (Robinson, 1968) which outlined the ways in which the polytechnics should distinguish themselves from existing universities. I had not been specifically attracted to the polytechnic by its emergent ideology. Initially, I taught English literature to students following the University of London BA General degree, but it was soon the policy of the polytechnic to develop its own degree courses. Course proposals had to be submitted for approval to the Council for National Academic Awards (CNAA). At the instigation of Eric Robinson, the poly-technic chose to take advantage of a new national award (the Diploma of Higher Education, DipHE) proposed by Mrs Thatcher's White Paper – *A Framework for Expansion* – in 1973 to attempt to embed a revolutionary con-ception of higher education (HE) practice within the polytechnic and the whole HE system by developing a course, underpinned by a philosophy, to lead to the new award. In 1973–74, I was seconded internally to be a part-time member of a development group. At the end of the year, the radical new

---

3. See, for instance, J. H. Muirhead, *Coleridge as Philosopher*, London: Allen and Unwin, 1930.

course was approved after difficult debate with the CNAA validating panel. In 1974, I became one of the first six tutors of the new course, run from a newly instituted School for Independent Study. I remained associated with this peda-gogical experiment until 1991 when the School was closed at the time when NELP became the University of East London after the national abolition of the 'binary divide'.

I have written extensively on the practice of 'independent study' at NELP[4] but there are several points which need to be made as background to the passage which follows. Firstly, I was completing my PhD in the first 18 months of employment at NELP. Increasingly, I sensed a similarity between the situ-ation of polytechnics in relation to the cultural dominance of universities and the historical situation which I had studied which had kept dissenting academies in educational, cultural and political subservience during the eight-eenth century. This sense was reinforced for me when I read M. F. D. Young's introduction to *Knowledge and Control: New Directions for the Sociology of Education* (Young, 1971) in which he suggested that the validation activity of the CNAA exemplified 'knowledge control' within British society. I spent several years arguing for the introduction of new courses, designed for disadvantaged applicants, in opposition to academic validators who would not accept that widened access to HE demanded alteration to the curriculum on offer. The pedagogical debate was also an epistemological one. The promotion of 'inde-pendent study' involved the conviction that the acquisition of knowledge is not the cumulative initiation into pre-existing disciplinary discourses but, rather, the consequence of the instrumental exercise of cognitive skill. I found myself attracted by the philosophy of John Dewey and opposed to the kind of epis-temological idealism exemplified in the early work of Karl Mannheim.[5] It was readily possible to advance this position within 'independent study' courses, but an acute problem arose when students graduating from these courses sought recognition for their qualifications within the UK HE system. The lack of recognition for students mirrored the opposition which the proposed courses had incurred when they were validated.

My years in the School for Independent Study (1974–91) involved intense course design and teaching. Throughout the same period, however, I tried to achieve some analytical detachment alongside my practice. I directed sev-eral research projects[6] and managed a research group with the intention of

---

4. See, especially, Robbins (1988) and Robbins (2020).
5. I particularly argued against Mannheim's doctoral thesis: 'Structural Analysis of Epistemology' (in *Essays on Sociology and Social Psychology*, London; Routledge, 1953). See Robbins (1981, 78).
6. Robbins, Adams and Stephens (1981).

demonstrating the validity of the pedagogic practice which had been developed. More personally, I tried to examine some objective correlatives of my experiences. Still with a view possibly to consolidating my association with the emerging 'sociology of literature' I initially studied part-time for an MSc in Sociology at the LSE to complement my qualification in literary study. By the end of this course in 1975, my interests had shifted from the sociology of literature towards the sociology of education and of knowledge. This had been influenced by my practice in the School for Independent Study. My experience was already showing me that social and educational changes cannot be achieved unilaterally through pedagogical innovation. Increasingly, my personal research interest focussed on the influence of institutional context on knowledge consolidation and transmission. I wrote an MSc thesis on the relationship between the development of academic sociology and the institutionalised department of sociology at the newly established University of Chicago in the 1890s and the early decades of the twentieth century. This enabled me to study Deweyan epistemology in historical context and it also focussed on the relations between the university department and the Hull House university settlement as well as on the articulation of a sociology of race at the time of the Chicago race riots of 1919. Another 'objective correlative' which was important for my thinking was the activity between 1940 and 1945 of the team at the École des cadres à Uriage which attempted pedagogical innovation under the control, at first, of the Youth ministry of the Vichy regime, and tried to sustain its originality clandestinely in alliance with the Resistance after 1942. In 1981–82, I had secondment as Morris Ginsberg Fellow in sociology at the LSE during which time I tried to coordinate the sociologies of organizations and of knowledge to generate a theoretical model for analysing the curricular consequences of objectively differentiated university institutions. My inclination was to use this model to argue for an extension of independent study across institutions such that students might opt for mobility between differentiated institutions to pursue their particular educational goals rather than remain trapped by the curricular orientation of one institution for the whole of their studies. For a part of my time (20 per cent) I was, from 1978, head of the European Unit of NELP's International Relations Unit, charged with promoting the institution's involvement in student mobility procedures within Europe. I argued in several conferences and reports to the European Commission for the development of part-course transfer between European institutions, requiring both the mutual recognition of standards and of cultural differences.[7]

---

7. Robbins (1978a) and Robbins (1982).

The essence of my interest in student mobility, both between institutions within the United Kingdom and within Europe, could be said to have been political in that I was committed to allowing students the opportunity themselves to manage their own self-development by accessing the culturally diverse institutions which could be at their disposal. It was predicated on the view that the curriculum content transmitted in HE institutions is culturally contingent and that the arbiters for their learning should be the students themselves. To use the terminology of Bourdieu and Passeron, it was predicated on the view that pedagogical authority is 'arbitrary' (Bourdieu and Passeron, 1970, 1977). This is an important reference. Initially stimulated by my reading of Bourdieu's contributions to *Knowledge and Control* (Young, 1971), I gradually found that the conceptual framework which he and his colleagues developed in their educational research in the 1960s was suited to my purposes in analysing and defending 'independent study'. To explore this further, I received a small grant from the Economic and Social Research Council (ESRC) to assess the relevance of Bourdieu's work to the analysis of HE institutions. I met Bourdieu in October 1986, and from that date onwards until his death in 2002 I remained in close contact with him and his team.

The meeting with Bourdieu rapidly became very significant for my career. By the end of the 1980s I began to fear that the School for Independent Study was losing direction. My partial detachment from its practice was legitimised when I was made a Reader in 1988. This enabled me to write a book, published in October 1988 (Robbins, 1988), which tried to re-state what I thought were the fundamental principles of 'independent study'. The subtitle of the book – *The Politics and Philosophy of an Educational Innovation, 1970–1987* – indicated that I was by then well aware that my educational actions during those 17 years were invested with political significance. I was soon to experience the way in which an educational innovation can be managed and suppressed through the political control of the institution in which it is located. The 'objective correlative' situation which I had examined through historical case studies became actualised. The period 1990–92 was a critical moment in the history of NELP. Within these years its status changed. It ceased to exist under the control of the local education authority, first of all becoming, for one year, 'incorporated' as the Polytechnic of East London before being designated the University of East London after the abolition, in 1992, of the 'binary divide'. During these years, the School for Independent Study was dissolved. From the autumn of 1991, there was no further student intake to its courses.[8]

---

8. With the exception of the MA/MSc by Independent Study which I had been involved in developing in 1982 and which continued after 1992 for a further decade exclusively within the School of Social Sciences.

The institution was intent on establishing its corporate identity within the market of HE institutions and could no longer tolerate courses which enabled students to negotiate their individual programmes of study. I was retained to help manage the progression of the existing cohorts of students (1991–93) and then I was found a position in the institution's School of Social Sciences. I was located within an ad hoc unit which managed social science modules which contributed to the university's modular degree programme rather than within the Department of Sociology. As at October 1993, I was forced to consider how to reshape my professional identity. I was no longer in a school committed to the advancement of student-centred learning but, equally, I was not required to transmit sociological knowledge. It was also the case that I no longer felt that the institution within which I was working was pursuing the political mission with which NELP had been vociferously associated. I had voted against the Conservative governments, from 1979 to 1992, particularly opposing the incorporation of HE institutions and the disparagement of sociology as Sir Keith Joseph operationalised Mrs Thatcher's famous dictum about society by subordinating social to economic science in the reorganisation of the Social Science Research Council (SSRC) as the ESRC. It now seemed, however, that my institution had surrendered and succumbed to the ruling ideology. I had never expressed my political position other than through my educational work, but this outlet was now denied.

During this period of transition within the institution I devoted myself to research on Bourdieu's intellectual development. This resulted in the publication in June 1991 of *The Work of Pierre Bourdieu* (Robbins, 1991). This research had a double effect. Substantively, it emphasised the importance in Bourdieu's development of the research which he undertook in Algeria at the end of the 1950s, showing that it was insufficient to regard him primarily as a sociologist of education. Rather, his sociological work had its origins in a philosophical orientation and in research fieldwork operating within an anthropological framework. The subtitle of the book was *Recognizing Society*. Through my work on Bourdieu I was beginning to transfer my previous interest in student self-determination to a more fundamental interest in social self-determination or social constructionism. I was beginning to believe that this fundamental orientation might be the basis for retrieving a society which might not be dominated by economic interests.

The publication of the book formally established my credentials as a member of staff within the School of Social Sciences. In my new institutional context I had to show that I was now able to contribute to the development of teaching and research in the social sciences. The paper which follows was one part of this process of self-legitimation.

In 1991, Phil Cohen set up the Centre for New Ethnicities Research (CNER) within the School of Social Sciences at UEL. It brought together staff in the institution who were concerned about new issues in relation to race and ethnicity. The notion of 'new ethnicities' was first developed by Stuart Hall at the Centre for Contemporary Cultural Studies at the University of Birmingham.[9] As Cohen subsequently summarised the new emphasis, 'The notion of new ethnicities referred to myriad forms of cultural traffic generated by the process of globalisation, and the convergence of transnational and transracial geographies of identification via the opening up of new diasporic networks of communication' (Cohen, 1999, 8).

During the time in which I worked in the School for Independent Study, my wife left her job in the Civil Service for a post in the Research and Reference Division of the Community Relations Commission, under the direction of Alan Little. She continued with freelance research on race relations after the birth of our sons. In the mid-1980s, she was appointed the UK representative on the evaluation team for the European Commission's Observatory on policies to combat social exclusion – the 'Poverty Programme'. By the early 1990s, therefore, the second-hand knowledge which I acquired in relation to UK race relations and the social policies of member states of the European Community combined with my growing interest in the social construction of state identity and membership. I visited Bourdieu and his colleagues in Paris in the early 1990s and followed eagerly the new journal – *Liber* – which he launched in October 1989. In a talk which Bourdieu gave in Brussels in March 1993, he indicated that his intention in establishing *Liber* was that it should provide a forum for the exchange within Europe of ideas about Europe. His intention was to 'historicise in order to disclose the historical conditions of particularity' as a basis for departicularising and universalising. This was especially necessary in respect of the different political philosophies in Europe: 'we need to carry out a study of this kind on political philosophy, one of the disciplines most closely linked to the particularities of the political traditions of each nation' (Bourdieu, 1993). Bourdieu wanted to provide a forum by which a sense of European identity might be constructed from the bottom up rather than from the top down. In this spirit, Bourdieu's close ally, Christophe Charle, had published a review of Brubaker's *Citizenship and Nationhood in France and Germany* (Brubaker, 1992) in *Liber*, No. 12 in December 1992, entitled 'France et Allemagne: Deux Politiques de la nationalité' (France and Germany: Two Politics of Nationality) . This was followed by an Italian contribution in *Liber*, No. 15 in September 1993, and by a Dutch contribution in *Liber*, No. 16 in December 1993. This was the context in which I volunteered to give a paper to the Centre for New Ethnicities Research in November 1993, which would

9. See S. Hall, 'New Ethnicities', in ed. Morley and Hsing Chen, *Stuart Hall – Critical Dialogues in Cultural Studies*, London: Routledge, 1996.

try to work from Brubaker's analysis to begin to develop an English response. My response to Brubaker was published in *Liber*, No. 19 in September 1994, as 'Citoyenneté et nationalité: Quelques Réflexions d'Angleterre' (Citizenship and Nationality: Some Reflections from England). A version of the paper was published internally in May 1995 as Working Paper 2 of the Centre for New Ethnicities Research, and it was revised for publication in 1998 in the *Journal of Franco-British Studies*.

Much of the argument of the paper was implicit or indirect, but there were two main targets. It found that Brubaker's discussion of the liberalisation of *standisch* distinctions – which generated economic openness but also indifference to state citizenship – resonated with my experience of the incorporation of the polytechnic. Secondly, my use of Habermas's critique of the English Revolution Settlement as based on the 'affirmation of ancient rights and freedoms' rather than, as in the case of the American and French Revolutions, on positivised natural law, revived my interest in the philosophical debate between Burke and Paine which had been the backdrop to my study of Coleridge's early thought. The young Coleridge had distrusted the abstract reason of Paine's *Rights of Man* and also the social conservatism of Burke's critique of that abstraction. He was feeling his way towards a social ontology, but this became his own kind of social conservatism that was readily embraced by the English Hegelians. The paper rejects T. H. Marshall's view of citizenship on the grounds that it is conceived still within a conservative tradition. It suggests that, in England, we 'need a definition of citizenship which […] seeks to start from a declaration of Human Rights', one, in other words, which follows from abstraction. However, the paper hesitantly suggests that a different line should be pursued – one which does not subordinate contemporary thinking about new ways of belonging to society either to an abstract concept or to historical tradition but which, instead, generates a reflexive sociology on the part of all citizens, including those who offer academic analysis. It recommends Bourdieu's socio-analysis as a way of combatting social exclusion.

B. The Text

Introduction

Many British people now experience difficulty when asked, on forms or in questionnaires, to offer self-definitions. The uncertainty is whether social identity is best expressed in terms of ethnicity or in terms of state membership. Within this main uncertainty there are two subordinate elements – whether state membership involves English, British or European 'state' membership, and whether ethnicity is too crudely represented by colour differentiation when 'Nordic' or 'Caucasian' possess more accuracy. These uncertainties suggest that there is every reason to undertake an analysis of 'Citizenship and Nationhood' in Britain along the lines suggested by the recent publication of Rogers Brubaker entitled *Citizenship and Nationhood in France and Germany*. [...]

I am drawn to the task by my involvement with the work of Pierre Bourdieu. Bourdieu has become increasingly interested in nation state construction and in the processes by which people are included or excluded from nation state membership.[10]

In his study 'L'identité et la représentation' (1980), he wrote:

> Struggles over ethnic or regional identity – in other words, over the properties (stigmata or emblems) linked with the *origin* through the *place* of origin and its associated durable marks, such as accent – are a particular case of the different struggles over classifications, struggles over the monopoly of the power to make people see and believe, to get them to know and recognize, to impose the legitimate definition of the divisions of the social world and, thereby, to *make and unmake groups*.[11]

Bourdieu's current intellectual/political/moral project is concerned with the articulation of differentness as a basis for integration, in opposition to official versions of 'integration' which are devices adopted by the powerful to retain their power. His European review of books, *Liber*, is an attempt to provide a forum within which European integration can be discussed on the basis of the articulation of national differences. In a recent paper, given in Brussels, Bourdieu outlined three principles of action designed to secure this aim of articulating particularity as a basis for constructing the universal. The first principle, according to Bourdieu, is that we need to

---

10. As well as of 'L'identité et la représentation', I am thinking here of Bourdieu's 'Le Nord et le Midi: Contribution à une analyse de l'effet Montesquieu' (*Actes de la recherche en sciences sociales*, 35, November 1980). I am also thinking of more recent Bourdieu texts: 'La Codification', in *Choses dites* (Paris: Éditions de Minuit, 1987); *La Noblesse d'État: Grandes Écoles et esprit de corps* (Paris: Éditions de Minuit, 1989); 'Esprits d'État' (*Actes de la recherche en sciences sociales*, 96–97, March 1993); and *La misère du monde* (Paris: Éditions du Seuil, 1993). *La Noblesse d'État* analyses the process by which an elite is constituted socially and educationally, which thereby possesses the power to impose a view of the state which maintains the position of that elite. *La misère du monde* is an attempt to enable those who are excluded from this state to articulate their self-understandings.

11. Pierre Bourdieu, *Language and Symbolic Power*, edited and introduced by John Thompson, Oxford: Polity Press, 1991, 221.

historicise so as to discover the historical conditions of particularity and, therefore, to provide the means to combat particularism, to departicularise, and, hence, to universalise. In this same perspective, the review *Liber* (which aims to set to work on this programme), includes a section which is called 'European ethnography' in which, by presenting detailed descriptions of institutions peculiar to nations – English clubs, German student associations, Swiss military service, Finnish firemen – we hope to make a contribution towards advancing the universal by demonstrating the historical foundations of particular national traditions which themselves are very often dispositions which are usually imputed to national natures or character. We need to carry out this kind of work on political philosophy, one of the disciplines most closely linked to the particularities of the political traditions of each nation.[12] (My translation)

[…] The intention, therefore, is to use the Brubaker book as a basis for articulating the differentness in cultural traditions of citizenship and nationhood in Europe.

I already knew of Brubaker as someone involved in the reception of Bourdieu's work in the United States. In 1985, Brubaker wrote an article in which, although generally in favour of Bourdieu's work to that time, he sought to expose some weaknesses in Bourdieu's theorising.[13] Brubaker had already explored the paradox of Weber's thought that, as he puts it, 'Modern man, then, cannot escape making a criterionless and therefore non-rational choice about the very meaning of rationality', or 'in Weber's view there is no rational way of deciding among the plurality of conflicting possible value commitments. Every rational life, in short, is founded on a non-rational choice'.[14]

For those familiar with the work of Bourdieu, it is easy to see why Brubaker's analysis of Weber should lead to an interest in him. Bourdieu's concept of 'habitus' – the notion that we all inherit dispositions to act and think in certain ways which we can modify but not overturn – seeks to offer an explanation of the origins of individual and societal non-rational choices of the rational.

Brubaker was a member of the Social Theory group which was formed at the Center for Psychosocial Studies in Chicago. With others, he was involved in readings and discussions of Bourdieu's work during the 1980s. Bourdieu

12. P. Bourdieu, 'L'Impromptu de Bruxelles', *Cahiers de l'École des sciences philosophiques et religieuses*, 14, 1993, 33–48.
13. R. Brubaker, 'Rethinking Classical Theory: The Sociological Vision of Pierre Bourdieu', *Theory and Society*, 14, 1985, 745–75.
14. R. Brubaker, *The Limits of Rationality: An Essay on the Social and Moral Thought of Max Weber*, London: Allen and Unwin, 1984, 87 and 98.

joined these discussions twice, and a conference held in 1989 led to the publication of *Bourdieu: Critical Perspectives*.[15] The contribution to this publication made by Brubaker is entitled 'Social Theory as Habitus'. Here he rightly argues that Bourdieu's social theory is strategically related to his social position and trajectory rather than definitive or absolute or 'true'.

Brubaker's work on Citizenship and Nationhood and also on Immigration and Naturalisation[16] mark his movement away from exclusively 'theoretical' writing to an engagement with a crucial socio-political issue. One of the interests of this text for me, therefore, is to consider whether, methodologically, Brubaker moves towards an analysis of society and social history in the manner of Bourdieu.[17]

As will become clear, much of the discussion in Brubaker's book hinges on the concept of 'citizenship' introduced by French revolutionary thought. My interest in seeking to suggest an analysis of the British situation stems from the fact that my doctoral research focussed on the work of Samuel Taylor Coleridge in the 1790s and this, in turn, necessitated an understanding of the social and philosophical relations between France and England during the period of the French Revolution. I shall come back to Coleridge later.

Finally, my interest in Brubaker's book is informed by my awareness of the work of the European Commission's Observatory on National Policies to Combat Social Exclusion. The Observatory brings together one expert from each of the member states. Since 1988 my wife has been the UK representative and I owe much of my knowledge to her work. Members produce annual national reports on both the processes which generate 'exclusion' in their states and on the policies which have been introduced to combat it. Much of the thinking of the observatory has been influenced by T. H. Marshall's definitions of 'rights' and I shall return to this later. Suffice it to say that the observatory is the locus of a struggle between competing tendencies, either to standardise, actually, and conceptually, social policy processes from the top down, or, alternatively, to articulate national differences with a view to universalising practice from the bottom up.

In what follows, I shall first summarise the argument of Brubaker's book, elaborating his account of the differences between citizenship and nationhood

15. P. Bourdieu, *Bourdieu: Critical Perspectives*, ed. C. Calhoun, E. LiPuma and M. Postone, Oxford: Polity Press, 1993.

16. See R. Brubaker, ed., *Immigration and the Politics of Citizenship in Europe and North America*, Lanham, MD: German Marshall Fund and University Press of America, 1989.

17. In passing, it should be noted that chapter 5 of *Citizenship and Nationhood* appears as 'De l'immigré au citoyen', *Actes de la recherche en sciences sociales*, 99, September 1993, an issue devoted to 'migrations et minorités'.

in France and Germany. I shall then attempt to sketch a comparable account of citizenship and nationhood in Britain. Finally, I shall try to suggest some shortcomings of Brubaker's methodology – shortcomings which might be corrected in a British account.

Brubaker's *Citizenship and Nationhood in France and Germany*

Although I believe this to be an exciting and important book, it does amount to a collection of essays which are rather uneasily put together. The book does not clearly advance a progressive argument and there is a great deal of slightly irritating repetition across chapters. I shall try to tidy this up a little by, firstly, summarising some of Brubaker's general statements about citizenship and nationhood and, secondly, extracting two coherent historical accounts of the developments of these ideas in France and Germany.

Firstly, the definitions. Brubaker's preface quotes from Aristotle's *Politics*: the state is

> a compound made up of citizens; and this compels us to consider who should properly be called a citizen and what a citizen really is. The nature of citizenship, like that of the state, is a question which is often disputed: there is no general agreement on a single definition: the man who is a citizen in a democracy is often not one in an oligarchy.[18]

What is at issue is the relationship between the territorial state, the definition of citizenship and the definition of nationality – as either synonymous with ethnicity or coterminous with territorial state membership.

The state is a construct which may often have been predetermined by physical, geographical conditions. Brubaker insists that an aspect of the self-construction of the state is the explicit distinction between its citizens and its non-citizens. He writes: 'Every modern state identifies a particular set of persons as its citizens and defines all others as non-citizens, as aliens.'[19]

He extends this statement to include nationhood: 'Every state claims to be the state of, and for, a particular bounded citizenry, usually conceived as a nation.'[20] In relation to these definitions, it is crucial to grasp the differentiation which Brubaker makes between France and Germany: French

18. R. Brubaker, *Citizenship and Nationhood in France and Germany*, Cambridge, MA: Harvard University Press, 1992, ix.
19. Ibid.
20. Ibid., x.

understandings of nationhood have been state-centred and 'assimilationist', German understandings ethnocultural and 'differentialist'.[21] His claim is that his book seeks to

> explain how these distinctive national self-understandings were deeply rooted in political and cultural geography; how they crystallised in the late nineteenth century and early-twentieth century; and how they came to be embodied and expressed in sharply opposed definitions of citizenship.[22]

[…]

Brubaker offers two geographical explanations for this fundamental difference between France and Germany. The first relates to their different legacies of medieval territorial organization – the different implications of the pre-existent French Kingdom as opposed to the pre-existent Holy Roman Empire: 'But while nation and kingdom were conceptually fused in France, nation and supranational Empire were sharply distinct in Germany'.[23]

The second explanation is based upon a view that the significance of the ethnocultural frontier between the Germans and the Slavs was different in kind from that of the ethnocultural boundaries within France.

> The French state did not fully assimilate Bretons, Basques, Corsicans, and Alsatians, but its failure was neither so complete, so evident by the turn of the century, nor so consequential for national self-understanding.[24]

These can only be said to be geographical 'determinants' in as much as early territorial settlements and social organisations in Europe can be shown to relate to the physical features of the continent. It is not possible to sustain a clear distinction between 'natural' patterns of social demarcation and humanly constructed distinctions, between the geographical and the historical, and the rest of Brubaker's account is concerned with the cumulative effects of human agency.

Before analysing the historical consolidation of the geographical, Brubaker has a chapter which clarifies the processes employed by states in relationship to citizenship. He distinguishes between two kinds of closure:

---

21. Ibid., xi.
22. Ibid.
23. Ibid., 4.
24. Ibid., 5.

Closure may occur on the threshold of interaction or 'inside' interaction. In the former case initial participation is restricted through barriers to entry or selective admission; in the latter continued participation is controlled through institutions such as probation or performance review.[25]

He proceeds to argue that territorial closure follows from the international state system, whereas internal domestic closure is essential to the modern state qua nation state.

He then gives other useful clarifications. The distinction between users and outsiders can be made residually or directly: 'The non-citizen is a residually-defined outsider. Every modern state defines its citizenship positively, in accordance with explicit, formally articulated criteria, and its non-citizens residually'.[26] Insider-outsider groupings, he suggests, may be temporary, short-term or permanent: 'Citizenries are insider groupings of the second kind'.[27] Definitions may be formal or informal: 'Closure based on citizenship is regulated by formally articulated norms', and 'Citizenship is an abstract, formal construct. [...] Yet formal closure against legal non-citizens may overlap in practice with informal closure against ethnocultural non-nationals'.[28]

In discussing Access to Citizenship, Brubaker makes the useful point that 'Citizenship is not only an instrument of closure [...] it is also an object of closure, a status to which access is restricted',[29] and, finally, he differentiates between two kinds of access to citizenship – by ascription or by naturalization, and, as he shrewdly points out, 'By restricting immigration, states indirectly restrict access to naturalization'.[30]

So much for Brubaker's causal suggestions and for his categorisation of processes and definitions of terms. Let us turn to his historical accounts.

France

The second chapter examines the changes made by the French Revolution to the notions of State membership prevailing in the ancien régime. Brubaker contends that 'Modern national citizenship was an invention of the French Revolution'.[31] Society during the ancien régime was essentially inegalitarian

---

25. Ibid., 23.
26. Ibid., 29.
27. Ibid.
28. Ibid., 30.
29. Ibid., 31.
30. Ibid., 34.
31. Ibid., 35.

and the determinant of one's rights was membership at a substate level. Citizenship was not an independent branch of the law.

> The pervasiveness of privilege in Ancien Régime society left no room for the common rights and obligations that make up the substance of modern citizenship. The distinction between citizens and foreigners had neither ideological nor practical significance. Foreigners suffered few disabilities, and the most significant of these, in the domain of inheritance, had been largely removed by the late-eighteenth century. Citizenship was not consistently defined or systematically codified: it was determined in an *ad hoc* manner in particular cases to make it accord with legal judgements about inheritance rights.[32]

The Revolution changed this situation, but its precise achievement can be viewed from four perspectives. By the view that long prevailed in French historical writing, it can be seen to have been a 'bourgeois revolution'. In this perspective, it substituted a common law for privilege (etymologically: private law), citoyens for privilégiés.[33]

Alternatively, however, the Revolution can be seen to have been primarily a 'democratic' revolution. The focus in this perspective is on the achievement of political rights rather than civil equality. Brubaker elaborates the grounds on which these two should not be thought to be the same. He distinguishes between citizenship as a 'general' membership status and citizenship as a 'special' status. 'General' membership was the construction of centralising monarchies which wished to break the power of feudal lords and corporate bodies. 'Special' membership was the creation of autonomous city-states. In general terms, therefore, Brubaker's view is that 'The modern state and state citizenship were constructed against urban autonomy and urban citizenship'.[34] It was the influence of Rousseau, however, which transformed this opposition and enabled the Revolution to appropriate the ideals which normally underpinned city-state membership in order to define the character of 'general' state membership. As Brubaker summarises cogently:

> As a democratic revolution, the French Revolution institutionalised political rights as citizenship rights, transposing them from the plane of the city state to that of the nation-state, and transforming them from a privilege to a general right. [...] As a democratic revolution, it joined the

---

32. Ibid., 39.
33. Ibid.
34. Ibid., 42.

substantive and formal definitions of citizenship, the classical Republican and modern conceptions. Attaching the content of the classical definition – participation in the business of rule – to the generalising, inclusive form of the modern definition, it made political participation a general rather than a special right. It followed the programme of absolutism in making citizenship a general rather than a special status. But it also followed the classical tradition in making participation in the business of rule, if not constitutive of citizenship, at least essential to citizenship.[35]

The French Revolution did not simply transform special rights into general rights. The rhetoric of the Revolution advanced the view that these general rights were the 'rights of man'. A third perspective on the Revolution, however, would see it as primarily a 'nationalist' revolution. In its early stages, it was both nationalist and cosmopolitan, but this balance could not be sustained. The Convention, for instance, arrested Thomas Paine. The consequence, as Brubaker puts it, was that 'by inventing the national citizen [...] the Revolution simultaneously invented the foreigner'.[36]

The Revolution can, finally, be seen to have been a 'bureaucratic' revolution and, in this perspective, the extension of rights to citizens as members of the nation-state was a means to securing the commitment of citizens to that state – as part, in other words, of a state-building exercise.

Having posed these different perspectives on the Revolution, Brubaker embarks on his account of the nineteenth-century modifications to the revolutionary legacy. The nineteenth-century debate which he presents was between the *jus soli* – citizenship rights claimed on the basis of place of birth, and the *jus sanguinis* – citizenship rights claimed on the basis of ethnic origin. Napoleon was in favour of an unconditional *jus soli* as an addition to the basic principle of *jus sanguinis*, but his view did not prevail in the construction of the Civil Code. In the final version of the Code, instead, children born in France of foreign parents did not have French citizenship attributed to them, but were able to claim French citizenship at majority. There were, therefore, 'actual' and 'potential' citizens, and reforms were proposed in mid-nineteenth-century France mainly because few people sought to transfer from potential to actual citizens under the Civil Code. Potential citizens were immune from military service without, apparently, suffering other disadvantages. The extension of *jus soli* was first proposed in 1831 and adopted in 1851. The law of that year declared French every person born in France of foreign parents, at least one of whom was also born in France. This extension to third-generation

---

35. Ibid., 43.
36. Ibid., 46.

immigrants was further extended to second-generation immigrants in a law of 1889. Brubaker shows that there were new factors at play in the debates leading to this legislation. The word 'nationalité' had entered the language and acquired an ethnocultural meaning by 1848; there had been a general criticism of French rationalism after the defeat of 1870 in the Franco-Prussian war; and there was the emergence of racist thinking exemplified in the work of Gobineau. Nevertheless, the extension of *jus soli* prevailed over the claims of *jus sanguinis* because of the Third Republic's confidence in its power to assimilate all citizens and as a result of its policies, particularly educational, designed to secure assimilation.

In brief, Brubaker's account leads him to conclude that

> The legislation of 1889 gave enduring form to the rules governing the attribution of French citizenship. Subsequent major revisions of citizenship law – in 1927, 1945, and 1973 – modified provisions concerning naturalisation, the effect of marriage on citizenship, and the attribution of citizenship *jure sanguinis*, but did not touch the principle of *jus soli* for second-generation immigrants.[37]

Germany

Brubaker's account of the historical origins of German conceptions of citizenship begins with the contention that 'central state authority developed in Brandenburg-Prussia around the standing army created in the mid-seventeenth century by Frederick William, the Great Elector'.[38] The centralising activity was not dissimilar to that practised in France during the ancien régime. There was the same inclination to break the power of special law communities so that, increasingly, the legal framework for the lives of people inhabiting the territory 'was set by monarchical administrative law, through the commissarial bureaucracy'.[39]

During the period of the French Revolution the *Allgemeines Landrecht* which had been prepared by Frederick the Great was finally enacted by his successor in 1794. It manifested a conflict between the natural-law orientation of the lawyer who was responsible for the drafting, and the inclination of Frederick William II to sustain the *Stände* or guilds/corporations. Consequently, as Brubaker says,

---

37. Ibid., 110–11.
38. Ibid., 55.
39. Ibid., 56.

The introduction proclaimed the equality of all before the Law, without regard to their *Stand,* yet the Law codified *standisch* inequalities. The title promised general law; the text articulated a mass of special law.[40]

Brubaker's view is that the *Allgemeines Landrecht* developed citizenship in three ways. It gave public, legal form to the military-administrative state. It increased state-centredness of law and membership, and it codified *Stand* membership, diminishing the extent to which it was hereditary. Brubaker concludes that 'the transformation of the Stände – from autonomous urban and provincial bodies into state-wide, state-constituted, state-regulated corporations – prepared the way for a more general state membership.[41]

That state membership, however, was based upon the liberation of closed economic corporations with the result that 'in the economic domain, persons met as free and equal individuals. But not as citizens'.[42]

A sense of state membership developed in Germany without reference to the notion of general democratic rights, which the French revolutionary thinkers had borrowed from Rousseau's thought. As Brubaker says: 'A purely liberal economy […] is indifferent to membership, to status. It is indifferent to the old *standisch* distinctions, but equally indifferent to citizenship'.[43]

His argument is that political closure in Germany was the direct consequence of the economic openness introduced by the *Allgemeines Landrecht*. 'The new economic openness ultimately required political closure; the destruction of the internally closed *Stände* required the construction of an externally closed citizenry'.[44]

In the seventeenth and eighteenth centuries, the state intervened to prevent the exclusion of the poor by municipalities, but the consequence of the liberalisation of *Stand* membership – combined with rural overpopulation – engendered a massive migrant poor. Legislation associated with the German Confederation of 1815 extended the bilateral agreements which had previously existed between particular states, now to include all states with a view to fostering freedom of movement. It was at this time that the concept of *Staatsangehörigkeit* (formal state membership) appeared in the treaties which were designed to regularise and coordinate expulsion practices. The culmination of this process of political closure was the codification of citizenship which occurred in 1842. As Brubaker writes, 'Prussian state-membership was

---

40. Ibid., 57.
41. Ibid., 60.
42. Ibid., 61.
43. Ibid., 62.
44. Ibid., 63.

codified as a means of shielding the state against foreign poor, whilst preserving freedom of movement within the state'.[45]

Nevertheless, in his view, large-scale immigration was not actual and did not seem likely for the first half of the nineteenth century. The citizenship laws adopted by the German states were based on *jus sanguinis*, but, he claims, this was not a reflection of any ethnocultural consideration. This holds for the common North German citizenship of 1870 and for the German Empire of 1871. At that date there was no hostility towards *jus soli* claims of citizenship, but, rather, indifference.

Brubaker's contention, therefore, is that, until 1870, there was a comparable attachment to a state membership attitude towards citizenship in both France and Germany. French citizenship, however, was formulated in terms of an expanding interpretation of *jus soli*, whilst German citizenship was based on the claim of *jus sanguinis* which did not yet possess any ethnocultural underpinning. It was in the period between 1870 and 1913 that the *jus sanguinis* position acquired an ethnocultural ideology.

Ethnoculturally, the Bismarckian empire was inconsistent. It excluded 10 million Austro-Hungarian Germans, whilst it included substantial non-German minorities – such as the French of Alsace-Lorraine. A dual policy had been adopted – of sustaining cultural support for overseas Germans and of assimilating domestically resident minorities, but this latter had failed in respect of the Poles. Whereas there had been some possibility of Polish assimilation to the Prussian state, after 1871 there was no possibility of assimilation to the German Reich. The era of the *Kulturkampf* saw a series of measures, starting with the Prussian School Supervision Law of 1872, designed to de-Polonise Prussia. Language laws followed leading to the establishment of German as the sole language of public life in Prussia in 1876. These policies anticipated the mass expulsions of the 1880s and the 'Settlement Law' of 1886 which committed state funds to buy up Polish estates and to settle German colonists on these lands.

By 1913, therefore, the demographic situation had changed dramatically from what it had been in 1870. The new law of 1913 was inclusive towards emigrants and exclusive towards immigrants. In 1894, the Pan-Germanic League had attacked the automatic loss of citizenship after 10 years' residence abroad, and the law of 1913 facilitated the preservation of citizenship by *Auslandsdeutsche* – those Germans living abroad. In doing so, the law severed citizenship from residence and 'defined the citizenry more consistently as a community of descent'.[46]

---

45. Ibid.
46. Ibid., 115.

In chapter 8, Brubaker swiftly takes his account of German citizenship up to the present day. He is able to demonstrate that 'the 1913 system of pure *jus sanguinis*, with no trace of *jus soli*, continues to determine the citizenship status of immigrants and their descendants today'.[47]

In concluding his comparison between French and German practice, therefore, he is able to remark:

> In France the civic incorporation of immigrants proceeds largely through the workings of *jus soli*, which automatically transforms second-generation immigrants into citizens. In Germany, by contrast, almost no consideration has been given to *jus soli*. [...] If *jus soli* à la française is unimaginable in Germany, this results in part from the lack of a viable assimilationist tradition. [...] Instead of a similarly effective and legitimate tradition of assimilation, Germany – like ethnoculturally intermixed Central Europe in general – has an uncertain and multivalent tradition of intercourse with ethnocultural others, a tradition with at least three different faces: one benignly differentialist; a second harshly (and thus often ineffectively) assimilationist; a third invidiously dissimilationist. The unthinkability of an assimilationist citizenship law in Germany reflects the lack of an assimilationist tradition and self-understanding.[48]

The British situation

I want now to try to sketch a British response which uses the categories developed by Brubaker in respect of France and Germany.

Clearly, the argument from geographical causality establishes a similarity between the British situation and the French in distinction from the German: that is to say that the geographical separation of the British Isles established the grounds for territorial statehood. Even though the nature of the incorporation of Scotland and Ireland into that British territorial statehood has been one of internal construction and a problematic one, nevertheless the development of notions of British citizenship occurred within a state-building framework without an ethnocultural dimension. The territorial separateness of the British Isles was unchallenged after the end of the cross-Channel activities which followed the battles of Agincourt and Crécy. The French and British kingdoms established themselves separately and simultaneously by the sixteenth century.

---

47. Ibid., 165.
48. Ibid., 176–77.

The political developments to which Brubaker would assign causal significance between France and Britain were, however, different. My guide in making this differentiation is the essay by Habermas published in *Theory and Practice* and entitled 'Natural Law and Revolution'.

Habermas expounds what was the essence of the revolutionary achievement of the French Revolution:

> The act by which the positivisation of Natural Rights was initiated, in America as well as in France, was a declaration of fundamental rights. As a consequence of the revolutionary self-understanding, this declaration had to give evidence of both insight and will; the insight into the rational coherence of the fundamental norm; and the will to establish the authority of a sanctioning power that was itself bound by these norms. This act of declaration had to make the claim that it was generating political power solely from philosophical insight. The idea of the political realisation of philosophy – namely, the autonomous creation, by contract, of legal compulsion springing solely from the compulsion of philosophical reason – is the concept of revolution which followed immanently from the principles of modern Natural Law.[49]

In other words – in Brubaker's terms – the French Revolution institutionalised political rights as citizenship rights by defining the rights of citizens abstractly or philosophically and by establishing democratic mechanisms which would operate under the same philosophically self-imposed sanction.

Habermas differentiates this achievement sharply from the earlier 'bourgeois' revolutions in the Netherlands and in Britain. Objectively these might appear to have been bourgeois revolutions,

> But subjectively the appeal at that time was to the preservation of the privileges of the estates [...]; for on the basis of classical Natural Law, violent resistance against the established government could only be legitimised in terms of the continuity of an ancient and at the same time eternal law, for example, the restoration, regeneration, or reformation of a tradition of law which had been interrupted. A century later it was still the landing of William of Orange and not the declaration of Parliament on the succession to the English throne which had given the Glorious Revolution its name. the Declaration of Rights itself was considered to be an affirmation of ancient rights and freedoms.[50]

---

49. J. Habermas, *Theory and Practice*, London: Heinemann, 1974, 85.
50. Ibid., 83.

In brief, the English had had a social revolution in the Civil War, but it was a social revolution which failed. In exile in France, Hobbes responded to the Civil War upheaval by elaborating a theory of social contract which legitimised autocratic rule. As Habermas indicates, the Glorious Revolution settlement safeguarded traditional privileges. The 'liberal' political philosophy of John Locke was one which upheld the rights of property owners – and incorporated the bourgeoisie into this settlement by extending the notion of 'property'.

Habermas was right to point to Burke's *Reflections on the Revolution in France* as an indication of the gulf that existed between English political thought and French revolutionary thought. Burke attacked the 'abstractness' of the rights elaborated by Tom Paine. Most of the English sympathisers of the French Revolution were, however, in fact members of societies celebrating the Revolution Settlement of 1688. The distinction between these rights and those advanced by the French Revolution was obscured by the apparent opposition to similar oppression which was generated by Pitt's suspension of Habeas Corpus. Most English sympathisers were defenders of the civil rights which they possessed under the Revolution settlement rather than defenders of the abstract Rights of Man. Burke believed that they distorted the meaning of the Revolution Settlement. His argument was directed against a sermon delivered by a nonconformist minister. Burke summarised the position of his opponent and then sought to demolish it:

> The political divine proceeds dogmatically to assert, that, by the principles of the Revolution, the people of England have acquired three fundamental rights, all which, with him, compose one system, and lie together in one short sentence, namely, that we have acquired a right,
> 1. 'To choose our own governors.'
> 2. 'To cahier them for misconduct.'
> 3. 'To frame a government for ourselves.'
>
> This new, and hitherto unheard of, bill of rights, though made in the name of the whole people, belongs to those gentlemen and their faction only. The body of the people of England have no share in it.[51]

For Burke, this interpretation of the Revolution Settlement as introducing democratically regulated, contractual government, was solely an ideology advanced by a class of socially excluded intellectuals. Even though they chose to assert new fundamental rights by reference to the supposed constitutional precedent offered by the Revolution Settlement rather than by reference to

---

51. E. Burke, *Reflections on the Revolution in France*, London: Everyman's Library, 1964, 14.

abstract human rights, nevertheless, their position was a threat to that of Burke. Burke insisted that the rights preserved at the end of the seventeenth century were those property rights and rights of privilege which sustained the existing social divisions.

It was the first generation of English Romantic poets – particularly Coleridge – that endowed Burke's conservatism with a new philosophical legitimacy. In spite of his early association with the radical supporters of the French Revolution, Coleridge's political enthusiasm rapidly expressed itself as philosophical idealism. It is not surprising that the ontological harmony of all living beings celebrated by Coleridge in *The Rime of the Ancient Mariner* (1796) should, by 1830, become the political ontology (to borrow the phrase used by Bourdieu of Heidegger) of the conception of the harmony of the landowning class and the permanent interests of the nation, sanctified by attachment to Nature. In 'On the Constitution of the Church and State' (1830), Coleridge argued in the following way:

> Now, in every country of civilised men, acknowledging the rights of property, and by means of determined boundaries and common laws united into one people or nation, the two antagonist powers or opposite interests of the state, under which all other state interests are comprised, are those of PERMANENCE and of PROGRESSION. [...] we have thus divided the subjects of the state into two orders, the agricultural or possessors of land; and the merchant, manufacturer, the distributive, and the professional bodies, under the common name of citizens.[52]

I am suggesting, therefore, that the romanticism which, in Germany, gave ideological substance to the ethnocultural conception of citizenship in opposition to French state-centred conceptions, in England provided an ethnocultural ideology for one sector of a split citizenry.

I want now to jump to the historical account of the development of 'rights' offered by T. H. Marshall in *Citizenship and Social Class*. Marshall distinguishes between civil, political and social rights in the following way:

> The civil element is composed of the rights necessary for individual freedom – liberty of the person, freedom of speech, thought and faith, the right to own property and to conclude valid contracts, and the right to justice. The last is of a different order from the others, because it is the right to defend and assert all one's rights on terms of equality with others and by due process of law. This shows us that the institutions most

---

52. S. T. Coleridge, *On the Constitution of the Church and State According to the Idea of Each*, London: Dent & Sons, 1972, 16.

directly associated with civil rights are the courts of justice. By the political element I mean the right to participate in the exercise of political power, as a member of a body invested with political authority or as an elector of the members of such a body. The corresponding institutions are parliament and councils of local government. By the social element I mean the whole range from the right to a modicum of economic welfare and security to the right to share to the full in the social heritage and to live the life of a civilised being according to the standards prevailing in the society. The institutions most closely connected with it are the educational system and the social services.[53]

Marshall claims that 'in early times' these three strands were wound into a single thread. There is no purpose to be served here in understanding when this supposed golden age occurred. Suffice it to say that Marshall argues that the three rights have historically been separately restored. He assigns the development of civil rights to the eighteenth century, political rights to the nineteenth century and social rights to the twentieth century.

The eighteenth-century achievement of civil rights was, according to Marshall, 'interrupted by the French Revolution and completed after it'.[54] The acquisition of political rights occurred gradually – as an extension of civil rights. Marshall writes:

> It is clear that, if we maintain that in the nineteenth century citizenship in the form of civil rights was universal, the political franchise was not one of the rights of citizenship. It was the privilege of a limited economic class, whose limits were extended by each successive Reform Act. [...] It was appropriate that nineteenth-century capitalist society should treat political rights as a secondary product of civil rights. It was equally appropriate that the twentieth century should abandon this position and attach political rights directly and independently to citizenship as such.[55]

Marshall interprets the acquisition of political rights essentially as the establishing of universal suffrage. He refuses to acknowledge the differentiating character of the French Revolution as Habermas has articulated it. For Marshall, the achieved reconciliation of civil, political and social rights in the Welfare State is the result of a process of evolution – an extension, in other words, of the

53. T. H. Marshall, 'Citizenship and Social Class', reprinted in T. H. Marshall and T. Bottomore, *Citizenship and Social Class*, London: Pluto Press, 1992, 8.
54. Ibid., 10.
55. Ibid., 13.

Revolution Settlement. Marshall's 'rights' are not rights at all – they are only the extended forms of privilege accorded to an extended proportion of the population by donors who tacitly retain positions which transcend the positions of those who possess rights. There is the sense that Coleridge's representatives of 'permanence' – the real stakeholders in the nation – release, as a form of patronage, 'rights' which will accommodate the representatives of 'progression'.

In the last 20 years, Marshall's work has been taken to be the classic statement of citizenship rights, and these have been the object of attack from the New Right. As Robert Moore argues in his foreword to a recently reissued edition of Marshall's work,

> For the authoritarian New Right [...] the idea of citizenship is a liberal absurdity that gives people ideas above their stations. It leads subjects to cease thinking of themselves as subjects and to believe themselves to be persons endowed with rights, rather than under the obligation to be governed. They regret the American and French revolutions, which celebrated citizenship.[56]

I am contending, however, that the argument between Marshall and the New Right is essentially an argument between the defenders of the Revolution Settlement and advocates of the German *Allgemeines Landrecht* of 1794 – the advocates of the freedom of economic rights without reference to citizenship rights.

Just as the German legislation opened the way for an ethnocultural definition of rights, so the encouragement of individualism within the market economy may leave a vacuum in citizenship thinking. I am suggesting that Marshall's view of rights cannot fill that vacuum because it conceives political and social rights as somehow the benevolent expression of a pre-existing civil society within which traditional privileges still obtained.

We need a definition of citizenship which, like that of the French Revolution, seeks to start from a declaration of Human Rights.

[...]

As a 'prolegomenon' to future work in this field, I suggest that we need to analyse the competing ideologies of citizenship and nationhood in relation to the social position of the ideologues. We need this nationally for each member state of the European Union as a prelude to understanding the process of convergence now occurring as Europe seeks to establish the rules of its own citizenship and nationhood. As Harold Perkin has written,

---

56. Ibid., vi.

Marshall's analysis is justly famous, but no one seems to have asked why he came to make it. It became so self-evidently part of the common-sense of twentieth-century social thought – even when that common-sense is under attack – that its provenance went unquestioned. Marshall was in fact a spokesman for the professional ideal as it applied to social policy.[57]

To eliminate generally the gap identified by Perkin in the case of Marshall in particular – to carry out an analysis of the provenance of the competing ideas of citizenship and nationhood – would involve following the work of Bourdieu more closely than does Brubaker. Such an analysis would expose the extent to which competing conceptions of citizenship and nationhood are themselves aspects of a power struggle. The implication for social action, therefore, is that social inclusion must develop mechanisms for enabling the excluded to include themselves conceptually within society.

---

57. H. Perkin. *The Rise of Professional Society: England since 1880*, London: Routledge, 1990, 333.

Chapter 4

BURKE AND BRISTOL REVISITED [1999]

A. The Background

During the period when I was involved in managing the closure of the School for Independent Study and writing *The Work of Pierre Bourdieu* (1989–92) my developing relations with Bourdieu and the team of staff in the Centre de Sociologie Européenne, Paris, compensated intellectually for my institutional uprooting at UEL. Through the 1990s, I attended some of Bourdieu's seminars at the École des Hautes Études en Sciences Sociales (EHESS) and some of his lectures at the Collège de France. I was invited to some of the research seminars and conferences which he organized. When I was made a Reader in the School for Independent Study in 1988, I had established a research group – the Group for Research into Access and Student Programmes (GRASP) – which supported pedagogical research. The group continued beyond the closure of the school. It was in Paris that I presented the findings of a project that I supervised, which compared the process of teaching economics between UEL's Economics and Business Studies degrees.[1] This pursued my interest in the extent to which the nature of the institutionalisation of a 'discipline' constitutes substantive cognitive difference. I pursued a similar line of enquiry when I next supervised a project which examined the correlation between the kinds of 'history' taught in institutions and the social position of those institutions within the hierarchy of the UK HE system.[2] I was exploring, in other words, the extent to which dominant institutions transmitted a perception of state membership to their students, whereas dominated institutions cultivated a subaltern ethos, or, significantly, whether some curricula conveyed a presumption of governing authority while others communicated a sense of excluded supplication.

---

1. Robbins (1992) and Robbins (1995b).
2. Robbins (1994).

While pursuing these 'Bourdieusian' research projects, I maintained my contribution to the work of UEL's European Unit by editing and contributing to its *European Up-date* bulletin. In this context, I extended my interest in the social conditions of institutional and curricular difference by projecting a comparison between the post-1968 development of the Paris 8 University which I visited at St Denis and the post-1968 development of NELP/PEL/UEL.[3] As a result of my connection with the Bourdieu network of researchers, I was invited to give a paper in the Frankreich Zentrum at the University of Freiburg, where I outlined a potential analysis of the teaching of history in European universities which would examine the institutional and cognitive bases of inter-university agreements within the ERASMUS scheme for student mobility.[4] In the same way as I had earlier proposed that the choice of further study for post-DipHE students should enable a conscious and reflexive selection of institutional context as well as course content, so I sought to propose that mechanisms for student mobility in Europe should encourage reflexivity about the cultural differences to which they were exposed. Both within the United Kingdom and within Europe, these projects and proposed projects were attempts to actualise the view expressed at the end of the paper on Citizenship and Nationhood – that the sense of state membership or of national or European identity should be constituted by citizens rather than superimposed by a ruling minority. For several years in the mid-1990s I secured EU funding to run an undergraduate module. I issued a summary of the argument of the module as 'Different Ways of Thinking about Society in Europe',[5] but this title does not disclose the extent to which the module was run as a participatory process. The module compared the post–World War II conditions in England, France and Germany, which generated the perspectives of Giddens, Bourdieu and Habermas as case studies of the social bases of sociopolitical philosophies, but it encouraged ERASMUS students taking the course to analyse and represent the conditions in their own countries which generated alternative views.

It should be clear that I was struggling through the 1990s to maintain a countercultural position with regard to the trends at UEL. I saw these trends – towards the commodification of knowledge and the marketisation of university institutions – as the consequence of the legacy of Mrs Thatcher's governments of the 1980s. My intellectual orientation and my impulse towards social action against discrimination both found more support in the circle around Bourdieu than in the United Kingdom. I found refuge and sustenance in France in

---

3. Robbins (1994b) and Robbins (1996a).
4. Robbins (1994a) and Robbins (1994c).,
5. Robbins (1996b).

particular and, by extension, in a Europe committed, under Jacques Delors, to social solidarity. My wife and I considered moving to France.

Things suddenly changed in 1997. Firstly, my work on Bourdieu started to become known in the United Kingdom. I was asked initially to speak at conferences which were mainly concerned with educational research.[6] I tried to take consideration of Bourdieu beyond the field of education in a keynote speech at the University of Southampton in April 1997,[7] and, in September 1997, I extended this further to deploy a Bourdieusian approach to the cultural field in which I had researched for my PhD.[8] At the same time, I maintained close contact with Paris. I tried to relate Bourdieu's thinking to some developments in British higher education policy in articles and reviews, and, in 1999, I translated, with Bourdieu's permission, some of his short texts. I was also preparing a new book on Bourdieu to be published by Polity Press.

Secondly, the victory of the Labour Party at the General Election of 1 May 1997, seemed to promise social change. I felt like the young Romantic poets had felt two hundred years before on hearing of the fall of the Bastille. This optimism on the national front was matched by my situation at UEL. Since 1993 I had belonged to a non-departmental group of teaching units but, in 1997, the university carried out a structural reorganisation and I was appointed to head a new department which would have responsibility for giving coherence to the existing units involved in teaching politics, social sciences (within the modular degree and outside the sociology degree run by the Sociology Department), linguistics and modern languages (French, German, Italian and Spanish). Within a year this department was formally named the Department of Social Politics, Languages and Linguistics (SPLL). I saw this as an opportunity to institutionalise some of Bourdieu's thinking. I tried to advance both his notion that the field of politics is socially constituted and his notion that sociolinguistics should be taken to be socio-linguistics, that is to say the study of the social conditions constituting linguistic communication. Similarly, I tried to argue that the study of European languages should become better integrated with an understanding of the different national cultures. Internally, I was intent on encouraging staff to participate in the construction of a departmental identity. We launched a series of 'Social Politics' working papers and validated new teaching units. I introduced one unit on Locke in which I explored the interrelations between political philosophy and the sociopolitical developments in England after the Civil War, highlighting the reciprocal relation between Locke's epistemology and his notion of

---

6. Primarily, a paper to an educational research conference at Bath in September 1995.
7. Published as Robbins (1999).
8. Published as Robbins (2000a).

toleration. I also introduced another unit on Kant which similarly attempted to correlate his philosophical position with the contemporary sociopolitical situation in Prussia. Meanwhile, I introduced a unit on Bourdieu in the anthropology degree which had recently been established within the Department of Sociology. It was called 'the Bourdieu paradigm' and it tried to emphasize that Bourdieu's fieldwork in Algeria deployed anthropological discourse to carry out philosophical analysis in the context of the confrontation of the Algerian war of independence.

It was the Politics staff who were primarily responsive to the challenge posed by the new department. The ESRC initiated a five-year research programme on 'Democracy and Participation' in 2000, and, as a team, we prepared a research application for funding. Related to this, we organised a one-day conference in June 1999, on 'Political Representation'. There were seven papers in total.[9] I gave the paper which follows. Other departmental staff participated. A French lecturer gave a paper on popular societies during the French Revolution,[10] and two politics lecturers[11] reported on a project which they had undertaken interviewing local MPs about their perceptions of parliamentary representation in East London. As a department we also tried to take advantage of the positive attitude being adopted towards Europe by the Blair government, particularly during the British presidency of the Commission (January–June 1998). We organised a seminar which was addressed by a senior civil servant and by the Austrian ambassador.

The purpose of these activities was to raise the profile of the department and to consolidate staff commitment. For my part, I had the sensation that I was again working in harmony with the orientation of the department which, in turn, was in harmony with the new political emphasis within the country. I no longer felt that my prime affinity lay abroad. There were three main elements of my paper. The first connection was unspoken and is apparent now only in the juxtapositions of this volume. In focussing first on Burke's famous characterisation of the status of the MP as proclaimed to the electors of Bristol, I was revisiting both my early work on the electors of Bristol South East in the early 1960s and also my understanding of the nature of the competing political philosophies which had been familiar to the young Coleridge. More significantly, I chose to consider Burke's position through a critical presentation of the interpretation offered by Ernest Barker (1874–1960) in a lecture which he gave in Bristol in the autumn of 1930 at about the time when Sir Stafford Cripps became MP in Bristol East. A significant part of my paper

---

9. External speakers were Ruth Scurr, Stuart Jones, James Connelly and Dick Pels.
10. John Whitworth.
11. Michael Keating and John Moore.

was devoted to consideration of the origins of Barker's conceptual framework. A subtext of my paper was that Barker's account of Burke was historically descriptive in character, showing little disposition to attempt a historical sociology of Burke's situation and no disposition to seek a scientific explanation of the class assumptions underlying Burke's notion of political representation. There was here an extension of the disquiet which I had expressed (as shown in Chapter 3B) about the analysis of citizenship offered by T. H. Marshall. I was tacitly feeling my way towards a critique of the political or social science offered by both men, the one (Barker) under the influence of the idealism of T. H. Green and Oxford Hegelianism and the other (Marshall) under the influence of L. T. Hobhouse (1864–1929), who was Martin White professor of sociology at the LSE from 1907 until 1929 but had also been trained at Oxford as a classicist at the end of the nineteenth century. My increasing commitment to the post-Durkheimian tradition within which Bourdieu worked was causing me to identify a homology between the traditions of English academicism and liberal sociology, one which had imposed both my intellectual exclusion and the relative degradation of the institution within which I was working. The important feature of the paper is only hinted at in the final paragraph. There are two undeveloped points which are made abruptly at the end of the paper. The first is the suggestion that, philosophically, Burke's theory of political representation corresponded with his mimetic theory of art and that both forms of representative thinking may, from the expressionism of the Romantics onwards, have become obsolete. The second is the tacit suggestion that Tony Blair's political philosophy derived from T. H. Green's belief that there should be 'no rights without responsibilities' and that the 'new Labour' movement was, therefore, based on an idealist moral philosophy rather than on a scientific approach to social reality. The concluding sentences suggest, like those at the end of the paper on citizenship and nationhood, that a new foundation for political representation is to be sought in a socio-analytic approach to the relations between electors and MPs.

B. The Text

I need to start by quoting the passage which will be the focus of attention for the whole of my paper. It is the famous passage from Burke's Speech to the Electors of Bristol which he gave on 'being declared by the Sheriffs, duly elected one of the representatives in Parliament for that city, on Thursday the third of November, 1774'. It is a key statement on Political Representation, one which, perhaps, has tacitly guided the practice of most Members of Parliament since it was first articulated by Burke. Bristol had just returned two Whig candidates, one of whom was a Bristol merchant with business interests in New York and the other – Burke – who was relatively unfamiliar with the constituency and had only been adopted as a candidate at the last minute after campaigning had started. Burke distinguishes his attitude towards representation from that of the other candidate:

> My worthy colleague says, his will ought to be subservient to yours. If that be all, the thing is innocent. If government were a matter of will upon any side, yours, without question, ought to be superior. But government and legislation are matters of reason and judgment, and not of inclination; and what sort of reason is that, in which the determination precedes the discussion; in which one set of men deliberate, and another decide; and where those who form the conclusion are perhaps three hundred miles distant from those who hear the arguments?
>
> To deliver an opinion, is the right of all men; that of constituents is a weighty and respectable opinion, which a representative ought always to rejoice to hear; and which he ought always most seriously to consider. But *authoritative* instructions; *mandates* issued, which the member is bound blindly and implicitly to obey, to vote, and to argue for, though contrary to the clearest conviction of his judgment and conscience, – these are things utterly unknown to the laws of this land, and which arise from a fundamental mistake of the whole order and tenor of our constitution.
>
> Parliament is not a *congress* of ambassadors from different and hostile interests; which interests each must maintain, as an agent and advocate, against other agents and advocates; but parliament is a *deliberative* assembly of *one* nation, with *one* interest, that of the whole; where, not local purposes, not local prejudices, ought to guide, but the general good, resulting from the general reason of the whole. You choose a member indeed; but when you have chosen him, he is not a member of Bristol, but he is a member of *parliament*. If the local constituent should have an interest, or should form an hasty opinion, evidently opposite to the real good of the rest of the community, the member for that place ought to be as far, as any other, from any endeavour to give it effect.[12]

In the autumn of 1930, Ernest Barker gave the Lewis Fry Memorial Lectures in the University of Bristol. These were published the following year with the title: 'Burke and His Bristol Constituency, 1774–1780', and this was one of the essays collected together and published in 1945 in Barker's *Essays on Government*.

---

12. E. Burke, *Speeches and Letters on American Affairs*, ed. P. McKevitt, London: Dent & Sons, 1961, 73–74.

Barker had taken up a new chair of Political Science at the University of Cambridge at the beginning of 1928, having previously been principal of King's College, London, from 1920. In that same autumn, Stafford Cripps, a new convert to the Labour Party, was appointed Solicitor General by Ramsay MacDonald and was found a safe seat in Bristol East. This occurred between the General Election of May 1929 in which Labour retained power only as a minority government and the establishment of a National Government in August, 1931 as an expedient to deal with the economic crisis that had brought about the collapse of the Labour administration – an expedient that was endorsed at the polls in the General Election of October 1931 at which the Labour Party was routed. Barker was giving his lectures in Bristol, therefore, at a time when a new member of the Labour Party, educated at Winchester and University College, London, was being given a parliamentary constituency in the town, not so much to represent the interests of his constituents as to legitimise his appointment to a high post in the Cabinet. He was giving his lectures at a time when the party political system was in disarray and was about to give way temporarily to a non-party government, partly so as to counteract the emergence of alternative parties such as that launched by Oswald Mosley in February 1931 – parties which were incipiently undemocratic. Finally, Barker was giving his lectures only a short while after the passing of the Equal Franchise Act of 1928. Whilst the Representation of the People Act of 1918 had abolished the property qualification for voting and enfranchised women aged 30 and over, the 1928 Act enfranchised women at 21 on the same basis as men. Systematically, plural voting arising from business or university qualifications was being eliminated such that the electorate as a proportion of the adult population was 90 per cent in 1929 as against 27 per cent in 1900. There had, in other words, been a huge statistical increase in democratic representation as a result of electoral reform.[13]

Set against this background, I want to attempt several different things in this paper. I want, first of all, to offer an account of Barker's thinking up to the point at which he gave his lectures on Burke and Bristol. I want, secondly, to look at these lectures in some detail in relation to Burke's own speeches and writings. I want, finally, to suggest that Barker's understanding of Burke was limited by the inadequacies of the conceptual framework that he adopted and

---

13. I am grateful for the information about Sir Stafford Cripps to the entry on him by Maurice Shock in K. Robbins, ed., *The Blackwell Biographical Dictionary of British Political Life in the Twentieth Century*, Oxford: Basil Blackwell, 1990, 108–11. I am grateful for the statistics concerning electoral change to K. Robbins, *The Eclipse of a Great Power. Modern Britain, 1870-1975*, London: Longman, 1983, 354–55.

that, therefore, revisiting Burke and Bristol differently might pose questions for contemporary issues related to Political Representation.

Born in 1874, Ernest Barker gained a scholarship to Manchester Grammar School at the age of 12 and then was awarded a classical scholarship to Balliol College, Oxford, in 1892. The first important thing to note, therefore, is that Barker studied Classical Greats. He gained a First Class degree in 1896, but, the second important thing to note is that he stayed on for a further year to study history and gained a First in modern history as well in one year instead of the usual two. He was elected to a Classics Fellowship at Merton College but, nevertheless, he was appointed to a lectureship in modern history, based at Wadham College, in 1899. He remained a lecturer in the Oxford Faculty of Modern History until his departure from Oxford in 1920. [...]

Barker's initiation into classical philosophy engendered a philosophy of history that placed limits on his historical analyses. Julia Stapleton has indicated that Barker was first exposed to the thought of the English Idealists as an undergraduate. She writes:

> He certainly absorbed Kant, Hegel, Green, and Bradley in the course of his studies for Greats. Equipped with this Idealist orientation, he developed an interest in the interpretation of political thought, if not in political philosophy itself.[14]

Barker himself recollected that the tradition of Merton College was

> primarily a tradition of the study of philosophy. Among the philosophical Fellows of my time the foremost was F. H. Bradley.[15]

These influences are explicitly acknowledged in the preface to Barker's first book, published in 1906. There Barker comments:

> My general conception of political science I owe to T. H. Green's *Principles of Political Obligation*; and it is with his teaching that I have contrasted, or (more often) compared, that of Plato and Aristotle.[16]

Delivered in the 1880s, Green's *Lectures on the Principles of Political Obligation* was published in 1895. They began with an analysis of the 'grounds of political

14. J. Stapleton, *Englishness and the Study of Politics. The Social and Political Thought of Ernest Barker*, Cambridge: University of Cambridge Press, 1994, 28.

15. E. Barker, Age and Youth: *Memories of Three Universities and the Father of Man*, London: Oxford University Press, 1953, 34.

16. E. Barker, *The Political Thought of Plato and Aristotle*, New York: Dover, 1959, vii.

obligation' which argued that the fallacy of Western European political philosophy from the mid-seventeenth century onwards lay in supposing that rights can be abstracted as 'human rights' from the social circumstances within which they are generated. As Green put it:

> The dissociation of innate rights from innate duties has gone along with the delusion that such rights existed apart from society.[17]

Following from this initial declaration, Green proceeded to expose in detail the weaknesses of the political philosophies of Spinoza, Hobbes, Locke and Rousseau. For Green, Rousseau most clearly demonstrated how far the positions adopted in this tradition of political thinking were untenable. By contrast, Green advanced a different view of government by consent. In a concluding section entitled 'Will, not force, is the basis of the state', Green contended that the political theories he had considered had all wrongly sought to understand or advocate ways in which political authority should be restrained or legitimised. He wrote:

> Looking back on the political theories which we have discussed, we may see that they all start with putting the question to be dealt with in the same way, and their errors are very much due to the way in which they put it. They make no inquiry into the development of society and of man through society. They take no account of other forms of community than that regulated by a supreme coercive power.[18]

What has to be accepted, instead, is that political authority is dependent on ethical ideals which develop within social situations. The political sphere is not legitimised by any degree of extended representation or suffrage. Its legitimacy resides in its conformity with values acquired within the non-political, social sphere. Green wrote:

> The doctrine that the rights of government are founded on the consent of the governed is a confused way of stating the truth, that the institutions by which man is moralised, by which he comes to do what he sees that he must, as distinct from what he would like, express a conception of a common good; that through them that conception takes form and reality; and that it is in turn through its presence in the individual that they have a constraining power over him, a power which is not that

---

17. T. H. Green, *Lectures on the Principles of Political Obligation*, London: Longmans, 1895, 48.
18. Ibid., 121.

of mere fear, still less a physical compulsion, but which leads him to do what he is not inclined to because there is a law that he should.[19]

It is clear that governments, for Green, must derive their authority from ethical values developed socially within those societies represented by the politicians, but there is an ambiguity in Green's position. It is not certain whether the constraining ethical values are absolutes deducible universally from social and community encounters or whether they are the products of changing social conditions. Green is sceptical about the democratisation of politics independently of morality, but it may also be the case that he is sceptical about what might be called the democratisation of ethics. In spite of the apparently Hegelian flavour of some of Green's remarks, his deference to the primacy of the social is fundamentally ahistorical. Political philosophy has, first and foremost, to be moral philosophy.

The consequences of this ambiguity in Green's work emerge in Barker's texts. As a philosopher turned historian, Barker sought to produce histories of political philosophy whilst retaining a commitment to a philosophical position which was ahistorical. This ambiguity is most apparent in Barker's introduction to his *Political Thought in England 1848 to 1914*, first published in 1915. Barker vacillates between a willingness to regard political thought as the product of contingent historical conditions and the inclination to regard political thought as an autonomous discourse, developing in relation to philosophical antecedents rather than in response to changing social conditions. After elaborating his commendation of the philosophy of Green, Barker tries to confront this issue directly. 'Political philosophy', he writes,

> not only advances of itself, and through its own acquisition of new, or restatement of old, philosophic conceptions; it also advances through the contributions of other studies, which can either supply analogies to guide its method or new facts to increase its content.[20]

He goes on to elaborate this position, first of all defining the nature of political philosophy in a way which indicates his allegiance to Green and his sympathy with English idealist thinking:

> Political philosophy in itself, and apart from other studies, is essentially an ethical study, which regards the State as a moral society, and inquires into the ways by which it seeks to attain its ultimate moral aim.[21]

---

19. Ibid., 123.
20. E. Barker, *Political Thought in England 1848 to 1914*, 5.
21. Ibid.

But, as Barker continues, 'other studies may influence its method, or add to its content'. *Other studies*, notice. That is to say that, for Barker, the impact of events or facts on thought has to be mediated by an intellectual conceptualisation of those events or facts. To be completely clear, I am saying that Barker does not really countenance the possibility that social historical or sociological analyses might directly explain differences in political thought. For him, 'other studies' simply provide additional information to be accommodated by political philosophy in such a way that political philosophy may still retain its fundamentally ahistorical, ethical basis. He briefly mentions Comte and the emergence of social science and he refers to historical method, and, finally, he explores studies which 'can add to the content of social philosophy'. By these he means biology, political economy, jurisprudence, psychology. After a short consideration of each of these new disciplines of study, Barker concludes:

> The moral nature of man is isolated in no vacuum; it stands in intimate and organic relation with physical structure and economic motive, with legal enactment, with social instinct, with historic or pre-historic institutions. Such relations social philosophy must necessarily consider. What it cannot admit is that any of the studies which deal with these other matters can solely or even primarily explain the reason and the value of society. They can throw additional light on the ultimate moral factor; in themselves they are necessarily one-sided and therefore misleading guides. They cannot absolve us from the primary duty of studying the State as the product and organ of the moral will of men.[22]

Before looking at Barker's application of this confused amalgam of historical and philosophical method to his analysis of Burke's relationship with his Bristol constituency, I want to demonstrate his confusion further by reference to his treatment, between 1900 and 1930, of the specific topic of Political Representation or Representative Government.

Barker's first book appeared in 1906 with the title *The Political Thought of Plato and Aristotle*. As Barker indicates in his preface, he had begun the book in 1899 as an introduction to Aristotle's *Politics*. The first text was, in other words, a product of Barker's classical education, at a prehistorical stage in his career. To introduce the work of Aristotle, he had found himself forced to explain the views of Plato and, in turn, those of the Sophists. The book expounded the autonomous development of Greek political thought, but it was not solely retrospective. As Barker puts it,

---

22. E. Barker, *Political Thought in England 1848 to 1914*, 6–7.

While thus 'looking backward', I have, in a sense, attempted to look forward. While attempting to refer Aristotelian conceptions to their sources
in past speculation, and to their basis in contemporary Greek politics,
I have also attempted to discuss the value of those conceptions to-day,
and the extent to which they can be applied to modern politics.[23]

In spite of the gesture towards a contextualisation of Greek political thought,
there is here little inclination towards relativism. Barker interprets Greek
concepts, but his attention to the social conditions within which they were
generated is minimal. The introduction to the 1906 text starts with an account
of the origin of political thought in Greece, followed by an account of the
Greek idea of the state. What is lacking is any historical analysis of the realities of political life within the city-states producing the philosophy. As a consequence, the argument becomes tautologous. The social conditions are not
mentioned so as to explain the nuances of the philosophy. Instead, the social
conditions are mentioned so as to clarify the origins of what Barker takes to be
the defining and universal characteristics of political philosophy:

> The detachment of the individual from the State, which is theoretically
> a necessary condition of political science, had already been attained in
> practice, in the life of the 'city'; and the Greek citizen, thoroughly as he
> was identified with his city, was yet sufficiently independent, and so far
> a separate moment in the action of the community, that he could think
> himself over against it, and so come by a philosophy of its meaning.[24]

Barker's text was, therefore, mainly preoccupied with Greek ideas. *The
Political Thought of Plato and Aristotle* went out of print just before World War
I and Barker set about a revision which he planned to issue as a two-volume
history of Greek Political Theory, the first to be devoted to Plato and his
predecessors and the second to Aristotle and his successors. In the event,
only one volume, entitled *Greek Political Theory*, was published in 1917. The
first chapter largely reproduces the introduction of the 1906 text, but there is
a completely new second chapter devoted to 'The Greek State' which deliberately tries to set an account of the emergence of Greek political theory
alongside the presentation of the facts of Greek social life. Barker argues,
for instance, that the Greek city was not a city and substantiates this point
in the following way:

---

23. E. Barker, *The Political Thought of Plato and Aristotle*, New York: Dover, 1959, vi.
24. Ibid., 3.

In the first place, it was not a mass of buildings or an urban area. The 'city' of Athens contained, on a rough estimate, the population of Bristol (the estimates vary between 300,000 and 400,000), and the area of Derbyshire. Half of the population lived in a central town, which was double, and contained a port as well as the inland town itself four miles away; half lived in the country. The whole 'city', including both town and country, was divided into about a hundred demes; and these [...] were individually centres of a vigorous local life, and active organs of the central government.[25]

With similar attention to detail, Barker offers new information about the 'Greek State and Representative Institutions', contending that the composition of the Council at Athens, if not the Assembly, was representative:

The demes acted as the local constituencies or electorates. The demes did not directly elect the 500 members of the Council; but each deme elected, and what is more, elected on a proportional system, according to the number of its inhabitants, a list of candidates – who, provided that they passed a test [...] of their qualifications, were duly eligible for selection by lot for a seat in the Council.[26]

It is clear that this new chapter represents, for the 1917 text, a significant attempt by Barker to historicise the text of 1906. It remains the case, however, that the philosophy and the historical context remain in uneasy juxtaposition. Barker did not have a theoretical framework that could enable him to analyse the philosophy in relation to the material conditions of its production.

I want to turn now specifically to Barker's long essay on Burke and Bristol. In 1930, what point about political representation was Barker wanting to make in presenting an historical account of the context in which Burke stated his philosophy of political representation? How far was Barker's account one which philosophically sought to endorse an idealist position, or how far was it one which used historical analysis to provide tools for reflecting on the changing nature of representation?

'Burke and his Bristol Constituency, 1774–1780' begins with a representation of the Zeitgeist of the years 1774–80. In a manner which, anachronistically, could be considered to be 'structuralist', Barker itemises a series of events or publications occurring within those years, implying a pattern of meaning

---

25. E. Barker, *Greek Political Theory. Plato and His Predecessors*, London: Methuen, 1960, 26.
26. Ibid., 39.

that may or may not have been experienced by many, or even few, of those living through the period. [...]

This introduction is followed by an account of Bristol in the eighteenth century – firstly an evocation of its topography, and then some demographic detail; and some suggestion of its wealth, based on its predominant share in the colonial trade with North America and the West Indies. [...] Barker proceeds to describe the affluence of Bristol, based on its flourishing trade. Social life bore comparison with life in London whilst, at the same time, contacts were very strong with the North American colonies and the West Indies, not least through the operation of the slave trade.

According to Barker's account, there were two Bristols in the eighteenth century – what he calls 'the Bristol of the Port and the city; and [...] the Bristol of Clifton and the Hot Wells'. The former was not only a city of trade and industry. It possessed a religious life of its own which, by the second half of the century, had become heavily influenced by Quakers and Methodists. En passant, Barker refers to the fact that Burke had been educated at a Quaker school in his youth and that the family of Irish Quakers had recommended him to the Bristol Quaker community when he stood for election in 1774, but he quickly moves on to digressions about Thomas Chatterton, a local vicar called Josiah Tucker, and an authoress from Bath called Catharine Macaulay, before returning to a description of the other Bristol, the socialite scene of the inland spa at Hotwells.

Barker moves on from an account of Bristol to one of Burke. I use Barker's summary of Burke's life both to introduce those facts and to comment on the way Barker glosses them. He writes:

Edmund Burke was the son of a Dublin lawyer, and he was born on the New Year's Day of 1729. His school was the Quaker school of the Shackletons, which left a lifelong impression and affection in his vivid and sensitive mind; his college was Trinity College, Dublin, where he spent five or six crowded years of rapid development from 1744 to the end of 1749. It is a college which has shown itself able to produce polymaths, who are not seldom tinctured by some degree of genius; in Burke it produce a genius, pure and absolute, who was tinctured by a more than respectable polymathy.

Burke founded a historical society at Trinity College, when aged 18, and in 1748 he produced 13 numbers of a paper called the Reformer which was largely about the Irish theatre. Barker lists the topics of some of Burke's known articles of 1748–49 and comments on a dozen or so of other articles which had recently been attributed to Burke, and he refers to the fact that it was probably in these years that Burke wrote a draft of what was to be published in 1756 as his *Essay on the Sublime and Beautiful*.

Burke came over to England in the spring of 1750 to read for the bar at the Middle Temple. He was never called to the bar, but two publications appeared in this period – firstly *A Vindication of Natural Society* and, secondly, as already mentioned, *A Philosophical Enquiry into the Origin of Our Ideas of the Sublime and Beautiful*. Through these works and through his contribution to the Annual Register, Barker suggests that Burke gained access to the post of secretary, first to an MP called Hamilton and then, subsequently, to the Marquis of Rockingham in July 1765, just a week after Rockingham had become prime minister. A seat in Parliament was immediately found for Burke and he became MP for Wendover. Barker comments on the fact that Burke had become acquainted with Dr Johnson and with David Garrick and was, therefore, still at home with the world of the theatre, and offers this as an explanation for the fact that Burke at once shone in Parliament at the beginning of his first session.

Barker next characterises Burke's association with Rockingham from 1765 until Rockingham's death in 1782, a decade and a half in which the Rockingham Whigs were only in power two times for a period amounting to about a year and a half in total. Barker details the position Burke adopted during this time:

> The passion for liberty and the zeal of the Whig tradition were upon him: and whether it were a matter of the rights of the electorate, as in the Wilkes case, or of the liberty of Parliament from the corrupting influence of the Court – whether it were the issue of American freedom from compulsory taxes, or of Irish freedom from commercial restrictions – whether it was toleration for Roman Catholics, or toleration for Nonconformists, that was at stake – he was consistent in the line which he took, and indefatigable in the ardour which he expended.

Barker goes on to describe the leading members of the party for which Burke became 'party organizer':

> They had great names: there was Rockingham himself, of the great Yorkshire house of Wentworth; there was the Duke of Portland and the Duke of Richmond; when he was not busy in fox-hunting, there was also Lord John Cavendish. Wentworth and Bentinck, Lennox and Cavendish – the names shine in our English skies: could anything more be desired?

Barker's quick pen-portraits convey well the contrast between Burke's dedicated political professionalism and the aristocratic dilettantism of his political masters, but there is also a touch of vestigial deference and respect in Barker's picture. Nevertheless, Barker's comment on the implications for Burke's thinking of his association with the aristocratic Whigs seems to rule out any suggestion of deferential conservatism. In the following passage, Barker gives a hint of the ideological lesson to be learnt from Burke's experience:

> Living in close touch with the grand seigneurs of England, he fell into a sort of contagious or induced temper of aristocratic thought. It was for the leaders of the people, he felt, to guide the people by their knowledge; it was for the people to find their leaders and to accept their guidance, imposing no mandates and giving no instructions, but leaving free course to a wisdom which was sovereignly conversant with matters of state. We may applaud the constitutional doctrine of the free representative which Burke preached to the people of Bristol; but as we read his correspondence we cannot but feel that he preached it with something of a mixture of professorial pride and aristocratic aloofness.

Barker closely charts Burke's relations with his constituents on the main issues of 1774 to 1780 – the issue of trade with America and the issue of religious toleration. More importantly, however, Barker locates Burke's view of representation in the context of the electoral crisis of the 1770s. In 1769, the House of Commons had banned John Wilkes from representing Middlesex in Parliament even though he had received more votes than the other candidate by 1,143 to 296. In reaction, Democratic clubs sprang up, urging electoral reform. Without accepting the platform of these clubs that there should be shorter parliaments, larger electorates and MPs acting under instruction, Burke tried to recommend a solution to the problems of parliament in his tract of 1770 entitled *Thoughts on the Cause of the Present Discontents*. Burke argued that there should be meetings in counties and boroughs to settle the standards for judging the behaviour of MPs, but, as Barker points out, this is not to say that Burke was in favour of a policy of instructions. Instead, as Barker summarises,

> it is a policy of watching conduct in the light of previously settled standards, and of remonstrating, after the event, whenever conduct fails to satisfy such standards; but it is not a policy of giving instructions in advance about the conduct actually to be followed.

Barker pursues this point to emphasise the nature of Burke's position underlying his speech of acceptance to the Sheriffs of Bristol:

When he came down to Bristol in 1774 this idea of free if responsible agency – we may almost say, free *because* responsible, when we reflect how closely freedom and responsibility are intertwined by the very nature of moral action – had settled deeply in his mind.

Notice here a point to which I shall shortly return – the way in which Barker glosses Burke's position as if it were the same as the idealist position of T. H. Green, advocating freedom with responsibility, rights entailing obligations.

Barker is impressed by Burke's conviction that an MP should be free and responsible, but he is aware that Burke was blind to the necessary processes of democratic participation. In particular, Burke was blind to the value of discussion within the community as opposed to deliberation within Parliament. To put this in Green's terms again, Barker contends that Burke was insufficiently willing to ground his political practice in the shared social morality which alone should legitimise that practice. As Barker elaborates,

Discussion, we may almost say, is the life-breath of all communities which in reality, and not merely in name, are free and self-governing. In itself, and considered simply as a process, it is an intellectual gymnastic which elicits and enlists the energy of a people's mind; in its results, and considered in the light of its product rather than its process, it achieves a common purpose, an agreed object (or system of objects) of the common life, a general will which is the peace of the whole community.

Burke did not have the inclination to engage in such discussion. He was prepared, as Barker puts it, 'to make the people felt by making the people feel' and this led him to be active in drafting petitions and encouraging consultations. However, suggests Barker, 'under this aspect the people becomes a sort of managed multitude'. In spite of the early influence upon him of the Quakers, Barker concludes that

there was one Quaker idea which he never really learned. It is the idea of 'the sense of the meeting': the idea of a union of minds, in a common purpose, attained through a process of general thought to which we may all contribute, and by a mode of amicable discussion in which we may all participate. It is the idea which underlies any grounded belief in democracy.

What are we to make of Barker's essay? What are the implications of his 1930 discussion of Burke's relations with Bristol between 1774 and 1780 for our thinking about political representation today? I want to give an outline of what I consider to be the fundamental conceptual inadequacies of Barker's article and I want to go on from there to make some concluding remarks which may have contemporary relevance.

Although Barker's article is polished and well informed, it is, nevertheless, bizarre that it is the work of someone who had only a year or so before been appointed to the first chair in Cambridge in Political Science. The article appears to me to be the product of a *belles lettres* tradition of social history writing. It is neither rigorous history of political philosophy nor does it show understanding of what might be involved in attempting more scientific social history or historical sociology. Although the consequence is here less blatant than in Barker's considerations of Greek thought, it is still the case that the supposedly detached account of the past is used in the service of a partisan purpose in the present. I can elaborate first in relation to the article as history of philosophy.

Precisely, perhaps, because Barker was seeking to present himself as a political scientist, the article concentrates on the political conditions within which Burke sought to implement his philosophy of political representation. The article says nothing about the origins of that philosophical stance. Both Burke's *A Vindication of Natural Society: Or, A View of the Miseries and Evils Arising to Mankind from Every Species of Artificial Society* (1756) and *A Philosophical Enquiry into the Origin of Our Ideas of the Sublime and Beautiful* (1757) demand some philosophical attention. From both works it is clear that Burke was very familiar with the work of Locke. *A Vindication* alludes to Locke's *Two Treatises of Government* and the introduction on Taste especially written for the second, 1759, edition of *A Philosophical Enquiry* quite explicitly engages with the epistemological positions advanced in Locke's *An Essay Concerning Human Understanding*. Burke was aware of the ambivalence – or, perhaps, contradiction – of Locke's legacy – that, epistemologically, ideas are dependent on sensations whilst, politically, reasoning is charged with the task of regulating feelings. Burke's *A Vindication* works through this tension. As a satirical tract, it simultaneously exposes the folly of political systems based on the exercise of reason ('artificial society') whilst ridiculing the idealisation of dependence on the expression of unrestrained 'natural' emotions. There must be some basis for action which is neither derived directly from individual experience nor from reasoning or abstract principles. Similarly, in *A Philosophical Enquiry*, Burke starts from a Lockean formulation of the problem in that he chooses to enquire into the origin of our *ideas* of the sublime and beautiful (by contrast, for instance, with Kant's *Observations on the Feeling of the Beautiful and Sublime* of 1763), but he is anxious to demonstrate, against Locke, that there are universal qualities of beauty and sublimity which exist independently of the relative human judgements of them. Burke begins the introduction: on Taste in the following way:

On a superficial view, we may seem to differ very widely from each other in our reasonings, and no less in our pleasures: but notwithstanding this difference, which I think to be rather apparent than real, it is possible that the standard both of reason and Taste is the same in all human creatures. For if there were not some principles of judgment as well as of sentiment common to all mankind, no hold could possibly be taken either on their reason or their passions, sufficient to maintain the ordinary correspond-ence of life. It appears indeed to be generally acknowledged, that with regard to truth and falsehood there is something fixed. We find people in their disputes continually appealing to certain tests and standards which are allowed on all sides, and are supposed to be established in our common nature. But there is not the same obvious concurrence in any uniform or settled principles which relate to Taste.[27]

It is the existence of a comparable concurrence that Burke seeks to establish. To do so, he goes beyond Locke's dependence on individual reasoning based on experience in ways which have implications for political philosophy as well as for aesthetics. All people, Burke contends, receive the same sensations of, for instance, softness and hardness, dark and bitter. Equally, because 'the power of the imagination is incapable of producing anything absolutely new; it can only vary the disposition of those ideas which it has received from the senses',[28] it follows that

> since the imagination is only the representative of the senses, it can only be pleased or displeased with the images from the same principle on which the sense is pleased or displeased with the realities; and conse-quently there must be just as close an agreement in the imaginations as in the senses of men.[29]

Notice here the use of the word 'representative'. As a faculty, the imagination represents the senses and has no capacity to vary what it represents. According to Burke, differences of Taste arise mainly from the exercise of judgement. He writes:

> The cause of a wrong Taste is a defect of judgment. And this may arise from a natural weakness of understanding […] or, which is much more

---

27. Burke, *A Philosophical Enquiry into the Sublime and the Beautiful*, ed. D. Womersley, Harmndsworth: Penguin Books, 1998, 63.
28. Ibid., 68.
29. Ibid., 69.

commonly the case, it may arise from a want of proper and well-directed exercise, which alone can make it strong and ready. [...] These causes produce different opinions upon every thing which is an object of the understanding, without inducing us to suppose, that there are no settled principles of reason.[30]

Finally, therefore, it follows that good taste can be acquired:

They who have cultivated that species of knowledge which makes the object of Taste, by degrees and habitually attain not only a soundness, but a readiness of judgment, as men do by the same methods on all other occasions.[31]

What I am arguing, in other words, is that Burke's theory of political representation was of a piece with his aesthetic position and that both were attempts to reconcile individual difference with an assumed universal commonality. For Burke, the electors were the Senses which were represented, as Imagination, through commissions and instructions, but the MP was someone who did more than juggle with invariable representations. He was someone who cultivated the judgement specific to the field of political action just as the man of good taste cultivated aesthetic judgements. My point is that Burke's philosophy of the political representative is predicated on a development within the tradition of empiricist epistemology. It offered a solution to the philosophical problems which Kant was to resolve differently in his Critical Philosophy and which the English Idealists, as post-empiricists and post-Kantians, were to attempt to resolve differently again at the end of the nineteenth century. Barker's presentation of Burke's position distorts it because it tries to impose a new epistemology on Burke's practice without seeking to understand the different epistemological basis of that practice.

My second criticism is that Barker made no attempt to offer a sociological explanation of Burke's career. The raw materials for such explanation are there anecdotally but they are not exploited. What I am looking for, and to put it in these terms is admittedly an anachronistic imposition, is an analysis such as might have been offered by a social historian such as E. P. Thompson. Barker makes reference to Burke's Irishness both in relation to his personality and in relation to his attitude to Irish political affairs. He also makes reference to the association between Burke's early Quaker education and his

---

30. Ibid., 75.
31. Ibid., 77.

relations with Quaker electors in Bristol. But there is no sign of an inclination to offer Burke's social origins, education and ethnicity as explanations of his political philosophy and political practice. Conor Cruise O'Brien's biography of Burke[32] goes some way in this direction, emphasising, for instance, the connection between the ambivalence of Burke's Anglo-Irish cultural identity and his incapacity to be an engaged political representative.

To conclude. Fighting against radical pressures to regard MPs as acting under instruction from their electors, Burke emphasised, instead, his view that Parliament should be a forum for the exercise of political judgement by those who had cultivated such professional judgement. The views of electors should only provide the raw materials on which judgements were made. Writing at a time when the proportion of the electorate to the whole population in the United Kingdom had massively increased, Barker still wished to celebrate Burke's belief in the rule of the educated, but he wanted to believe that the legitimacy of this rule could emerge, almost metaphysically, out of the will of the community. He imposed idealist political philosophy and ethics on an ideology that was based on empiricism. I am wanting to suggest that there is at the moment a crisis of thinking in respect of political representation because there are strengths in Green's rejection of Rousseauistic direct representation whilst, at the same time, no shared philosophical basis for accepting the judgement of those returned to deliberate in Parliament. In responding to Barker on Burke, I am suggesting that Barker's analysis fails because his social historical methodology is unsatisfactory. I have sympathy with his emphasis on the primacy of the social, but he still – in spite of Green's injunctions – conceptualised the relationship between the social and the political dualistically. Although he argued that, as a political professional, Burke should have remained more in tune with his social constituents, Barker still conceived political representation as a mimetic activity. Politics represents society, or politicians represent the social in the same way as, in the eighteenth century, Art represented Nature. Although adopting Green's post-empirical moral philosophy, Barker still thought within the framework of the British empirical tradition as much as had Burke. Aesthetically, we have moved from mimetic theory through romanticism, impressionism, abstract expressionism to conceptual art. For contemporary artists, art is about installations and interventions more than about representation. By analogy, we may now need to move towards an understanding that politicians do not operate in an autonomous sphere in which they seek to re-present the view of those they represent. Instead, politicians need to be understood as social agents operating within a particular sphere of

---

32. C. O'Brien, *The Great Melody: A Thematic Biography and Commented Anthology of Edmund Burke*, London: Sinclair-Stevenson, 1992.

activity. As such, we need to move to the situation where we choose MPs not so much in terms of the political opinions they adopt publicly but more in terms of an awareness of their social attitudes – attitudes as dispositions to act which can be predicted by reference to a sociological understanding of their origins and life trajectories. Electoral choice might then be given new life because it would acknowledge the social dynamism of political action and not be locked in the static, reactive, representative model.

Chapter 5

FROM SOLIDARITY TO SOCIAL INCLUSION: THE POLITICAL TRANSFORMATIONS OF DURKHEIMIANISM [2008]

A. The Background

The turn of the century was the high point of my close working relations with Bourdieu and his colleagues. In 1999, I translated 'Sur les ruses de la raison impérialiste' (On the Cunning of Imperialist Reason) – an article that Bourdieu had co-authored with Loïc Wacquant which argued that dualistic American conceptions of race had been imposed on a Latin American situation which was multiracial.[1] The following year, the book on Bourdieu which I had commenced for Polity Press was accepted and published by Sage.[2] Meanwhile, I was preparing, also for publication by Sage, a four-volume collection of articles on Bourdieu's work.[3] Bourdieu gave me access to his personal collection of secondary texts to assist me in this editorial process. In October 2000, I organised a conference on Bourdieu's work at UEL ('Bourdieu in the 21st Century').

This phase came to an end with Bourdieu's death in April 2002. Before his death, I had indicated that I wanted to develop a transnational project on conceptual transfer between France and the United Kingdom. This arose from my awareness, from personal experience, of the difficulties of communicating Bourdieu's ideas within the English intellectual field. He suggested that I should collaborate with Dominique Merrlié[4] to explore, as a case study, the social conditions of the production of the work of Lucien Lévy-Bruhl[5] and

---

1. Bourdieu and Wacquant, 1998; Bourdieu and Wacquant, 1999.
2. Robbins (2000a).
3. Robbins (2000c).
4. Dominique Merrlié, editor of a special number of the *Revue Philosophique de la France et de l'Étranger* celebrating the fiftieth anniversary of Lévy-Bruhl's death: 'Autour de Lucien Lévy-Bruhl', 1989, 4
5. Lucien Lévy-Bruhl (1857–1939).

of its reception in the United Kingdom. We gained a Franco-British research grant, funded by the British Academy and the CNRS, for a series of seminars which took place, alternating between France and the United Kingdom, from 2002 to 2004. In preparation for the research application, I read Lévy-Bruhl's work systematically and there were two immediate spin-offs. I translated an extract on Leibniz from Lévy-Bruhl's *Allemagne depuis Leibniz* (1890),[6] and I gave a paper, in November 2001, on 'Lévy-Bruhl's representation of Comte' at a seminar organised by the Institute of Social and Cultural Anthropology and the Maison Française, University of Oxford. Highlighting Lévy-Bruhl's account of the work of Leibniz, I first illustrated the way in which he had analysed the sociopolitical conditions of the production of philosophy in Germany in the eighteenth century. The second was an opportunity for me to consider the way in which Lévy-Bruhl used the same approach in representing the emerging social science of Comte – the social science which constituted the framework for Lévy-Bruhl's own formation as well as for that of his contemporary, Durkheim. Between 2002 and 2004 I gave a paper at each of the four joint seminars of the project.[7] These seminars provided the chance to examine the cross-national transfer of ideas between the French and English intellectual traditions in the period between 1900 and 1940. Perhaps more importantly, they introduced me to the substance of Lévy-Bruhl's thought, enabling me to understand more adequately his much maligned notion of 'primitive mentality'. Additionally, the project introduced me to the activities of the Centre for Durkheimian Studies. I gave a further paper at one of its study days[8] and this led to the invitation to give a speech at the conference organised by the Centre to commemorate the 150th anniversary of Durkheim's birth. This is the paper which follows.

Working on Lévy-Bruhl reinforced the awareness which I had already derived from Bourdieu's reflections on his anthropological research in Algeria of the tendency of Western thought to impose a model of rational behaviour on actions in precolonial societies. Before Bourdieu's death, I spent time in Paris transcribing and translating the unpublished part of Foucault's doctoral thesis which had been a commentary on his published translation of Kant's late *Anthropologie in pragmatischer*

---

6. Robbins (2001).
7. September 2002: 'Georges Davy's representation of Lucien Lévy-Bruhl'; November 2002: 'Some notes on the English translations and English reception of Lévy-Bruhl's work during his lifetime'; September 2003: 'Quelques remarques sur Lévy-Bruhl, Husserl et Levinas'; November 2003: 'Lévy-Bruhl, Robin Horton and modes of thought', all unpublished.
8. Published as Robbins (2003).

Hinsicht.[9] Foucault's text raised the question whether Kant's pragmatic anthropology was invalidated by its dependence on his earlier critical epistemology, thus suggesting the need, instead, for a phenomenological pragmatism, an exploration of social realities without a priori assumptions. I also experienced in this period some practical examples of this methodological issue. In 1999, I spent a week in Harare, Zimbabwe, to explore the possibility that students taking courses there run by the Tavistock Clinic, London, on family psychiatry might complete their studies to degree level and beyond by 'independent study' undertaken remotely.[10] I observed the encounter which this process would entail between the traditional family values of Shona culture and Western assumptions about psychiatric norms. Additionally, in the early years of the century, I was a member of the supervisory team for a Kenyan PhD student who was researching the effects of World Bank funding, with its assumptions about state social care systems, on tribal processes of community self-help in his own country.

These were all factors which caused me to become primarily interested in the cross-cultural transfer of concepts, at first in respect of Franco-British transfer and then in respect of transfer from the West to other countries in the world. The death of Bourdieu inevitably initiated a new phase in my work. I was no longer part of his network or entourage and I therefore found myself necessarily adopting a detached stance towards the inter-national communication process in which I had been immersed. Other developments encouraged this detachment. In 2001, UEL carried out a structural reorganisation in order to remain solvent. It was thought no longer possible to support the teaching of foreign languages. The Department of Social Politics, Languages and Linguistics was closed. I was given a sabbatical and also appointed a professor. I took the opportunity to attempt to launch a research orientation which would prolong Bourdieu's project without myself being obliged to behave just as an acolyte. I gave a paper at the conference in Paris which commemorated Bourdieu in January 2003,[11] and I organised a conference entitled 'Social Science Beyond Bourdieu' at UEL in June 2003, but I had already given an inaugural lecture in April 2002, entitled: 'Finding "reasons for maxims": social

---

9. At the time I was not given permission to publish my translation on the grounds that publication would contravene the terms of Foucault's will, but this has since been ignored and the text has been published as Foucault, 2008.
10. UEL had a close association with the Tavistock Clinic. The MA/MSc by independent study which had been validated in 1980 within the School for Independent Study survived the closure of the school, continuing solely within the School of Social Sciences.
11. 'L'échange intellectuelle anglo-française pendant les années 1965 à 1980', unpublished.

science and international relations',[12] and established a research group called the Group for the Study of International Social Science.

My work on Foucault's commentary on Kant led me to become associated with the Société d'Études Kantiennes de Langue Française. I gave papers at its annual conferences in 2004 and 2005. In both papers, rather against the grain of the society, I tried to consider Kant's work sociologically rather than in terms of philosophical discourse.[13] This led me to make several research applications, either to compare the French and English reception of Kant in the nineteenth century and the differential consequences for the development of social science in the two countries or, more specifically, to analyse the work of the main nineteenth-century translator of Kant into French – J. Tissot. These two research applications were unsuccessful, but I continued my attempt to understand those philosophical orientations in the French intellectual tradition which differentiated Bourdieu's research from British empirical sociology. After the successful publication of the four-volume collection of essays on Bourdieu, Sage asked me to compile a similar collection on Jean-François Lyotard in its Masters of Contemporary Thought series. This was published, in three volumes, in April 2004.[14] This caused me to study Lyotard's work systematically, particularly his early introduction to phenomenology,[15] his *La condition postmoderne*,[16] and his later analyses of Kant.[17] In previous years I had examined the influence on Bourdieu's thinking of, in particular, Leibniz, Kant and Cassirer, and I knew that Bourdieu had been hostile to postmodernism, but I now became alert to the perspective on the phenomenological movement offered by Lyotard in the book published when Bourdieu was a student and also to the coincidence that Lyotard was reporting on the political situation in Algeria for *Socialisme ou Barbarie* at the same time that Bourdieu was undertaking his fieldwork there. In 2006–7, I co-organized, with Nirmal Puwar and Azzedine Haddour, an ESRC Research Seminar Series entitled 'Thinking with Pierre Bourdieu in Algeria: Testimonies of Uprooting'. I gave two papers in this series, the first of which specifically explored the French reception of Husserl's phenomenology in the 1950s,[18] and the second of which considered

---

12. See Robbins (2006a, 233–49).
13. The papers were published in the proceedings for the two conferences: Robbins (2005, 2009a).
14. Robbins (2004). My editor's introduction was entitled 'From postwar to postmodern. Lyotard's "interregnum" and after'.
15. Lyotard (1954).
16. Lyotard (1979, 1986a)
17. Lyotard (1986b, 1991, 1994)
18. D. Robbins, 'Some Notes on the French Reception of the Work of Husserl', March 2007, unpublished.

the extent to which Bourdieu's putative phenomenological analysis of cross-cultural relations within Algeria was in fact pre-conceptualised by perspectives derived from Durkheim and Weber as well as from the anthropological record established by nineteenth-century French colonial administrators.[19]

During these years, members of the Group for the Study of International Social Science organised a series of internal seminars, some of which examined in detail the 'crisis' thinking in Europe in the 1930s, to which I contributed a paper discussing Bourdieu's article and book on the political ontology of Martin Heidegger. From 2005 to 2007 I was PhD co-ordinator in what had now become the School of Social Sciences, Media and Cultural Studies following a merger of the Schools of Social Sciences and Cultural and Innovation Studies. It suited me well to organise supporting seminars for research students which would raise the issue of 'inter-disciplinarity' in research practice. I organised the publication of an annual bulletin of PhD research in progress in the school by which I sought to establish the ethos of a postgraduate community modelled on Bourdieu's management of the Centre de Sociologie Européenne and his editing of the *Actes de la recherche en sciences sociales*. The first two yearbooks were published in September 2007, the third in June 2009. A fourth, published in September 2009, inaugurated a new series entitled Crossing Conceptual Boundaries for which I wrote 'Publication: A Theoretical Preamble' in which I discussed the status and function of the bulletins.[20] These publications correlated with the way in which I had, in 2006, edited a special number of the journal *Theory, Culture & Society*[21] on the work of Bourdieu in which I solicited contributions from European colleagues with a view to disclosing alternative cultural approaches to the question of 'judgement', deliberately referencing Bourdieu's own 'Towards a vulgar critique of judgement'. In these instances, I was trying to emphasise that research enquiry of cultural criticism should occur in terms of the original predispositions of the researchers or critics rather than in relation to the predefined frames of thought provided by intellectual 'disciplines'. In Bourdieu's terms, I was trying to maintain the notion that understanding corresponds with the 'structuring structures' of thought rather than tautologously within 'structured structures'. Also, in 2006 I published a collection of my publications to that date under the title: *On Bourdieu, Education and Society*.[22] Most importantly, this collection was prefaced by a long introduction in which I made explicit, adopting a phenomenological orientation, the cultural dispositions which had shaped my interpretations of

---

19. D. Robbins, 'Religion and Cultural Politics', May 2007, unpublished.
20. Robbins (2009b).
21. Robbins (2006b).
22. Robbins (2006a).

the work of Bourdieu. The *Theory, Culture & Society* special number was followed by a seminar in which most of the contributors exchanged views. Similarly, I used the postgraduate student bulletins to try to widen the student research community so as to ensure that it did not remain introvertedly situated within the social situation of UEL. In one respect, this was already guaranteed by the multinational character of the student group, but I set up a channel of communication with research students in Marseille so as to make explicit the ways in which the practice of research is framed by the different cultural contexts within which it is undertaken.

The involvement of research students from Marseille was a by-product of a development in my career which initially ran alongside my responsibility for PhD students in my school. In 2003, Jean-Claude Passeron had been the main guest speaker at the 'Social Science beyond Bourdieu' conference. Contact with him showed me the similarities and dissimilarities between his work and career and those of Bourdieu. I was particularly interested in his decision to become Head of the Department of Sociology in 1968 at the 'experimental university' at Vincennes (to become Paris 8) after a decade of collaboration with Bourdieu on educational research. There seemed to be an opportunity for me to develop a detached perspective on Bourdieu's work by comparing his trajectory with that of Passeron. I first applied in 2006 for an ESRC grant to make a comparison between the work of the two men, but a resubmitted application was only successful a year later when I revised the proposal to concentrate entirely on an exposition of the work of Passeron.[23] In retirement, Passeron was still closely associated with SHADyC,[24] a research group which he had founded and which was based in Marseille. My research project involved research visits to Marseille, interviews, seminars and conferences in which Passeron participated. For a short while, these contacts enabled me to develop links between research students at UEL and those in Marseille. A proportion of Yearbook III of June 2009 focussed on cross-cultural collaboration and on comparison between the meanings of 'culture' in the two countries. The project culminated in a translated edition of Passeron's main book – *Le raisonnement sociologique* as *Sociological Reasoning*[25] – with an introduction in which I tried to compare the methodologies of the two men.

Starting from my first visit to Marseille in the autumn of 2007, I began to appreciate in a new way some of the characteristics of Passeron's specific

---

23. 'The work of Jean-Claude Passeron, 1960–present: A case-study analysis of the development of a philosophy of social science' (Ref: RES-000-22-2494).
24. Sociologie, Histoire, Anthropologie des Dynamiques Culturelles [the Sociology, History, and Anthropology of Cultural Dynamics].
25. Passeron (2013 [1991]).

contributions to the work of the Centre de Sociologie Européenne (CSE) and
to the texts which he co-authored with Bourdieu in the 1960s. Firstly, Passeron's
understanding of sociological explanation was that it is totally rooted within
the historical conditions of its production. Passeron was interested in the relative status of concepts in philosophical and sociological discourse, insisting
that sociological concepts have no a priori, logical status. Related to this conviction was Passeron's constant reflection on the relationship between learned
and popular knowledge, indicated in part by his friendship with Richard
Hoggart. I gave especial attention to the book which Passeron co-authored
with Claude Grignon entitled *Le savant et le populaire*[26] (The Scientist and the
Ordinary Person) and to the textbook for research students called *Le métier de
sociologue*[27] (The Craft of Sociology) which he and Bourdieu wrote in collaboration with Jean-Claude Chamboredon in which they agreed that sociological
knowledge advances through experiment and testing in constantly changing
circumstances without ever acquiring any transcendent truth.

Several key themes from my earlier work are interwoven in the text which
follows. It was a paper which offered a scholarly interpretation of Durkheim's
work in commemoration of the 150th anniversary of his death, but it was also
a partisan polemic.

Firstly, it seized on a suggestion made by Watts Miller, in his then recently
published English translation of Durkheim's Latin doctoral thesis, that
Durkheim's endeavour at first was to offer social science as a science which
superseded political science or political philosophy. I was trying to harness
Durkheim's work in support of an elevation of the social and the subordination of the political. Secondly, it wanted to argue, using the article by Alpert,
that Durkheim saw social science as an instrument for social action, promoted
through pedagogical communication within transformed university institutions.
This was a retrospective justification of all of my own pedagogic practices – in
the School for Independent Study, in 'Social Politics', and in the cultivation of
a postgraduate research community designed to articulate cross-cultural conceptual exchange. This was a view which was consonant with Bourdieu and
Passeron's insistence that social science is to be deployed in action rather than
accumulated as knowledge in social detachment. It also corresponded with my
interpretation of the relationship between theory and practice at the turn of
the nineteenth century when the Department of Sociology was instituted in
the newly established University of Chicago. Thirdly, the paper went further.
It suggested, using T. N. Clark's book, that Durkheim's intention that social
science should be the foundation for a communitarian usurpation of political

---

26. Passeron and Grignon (1989).
27. Bourdieu, Chamboredon and Passeron (1968, 1991).

authority was suppressed after his death (in 1917) by the 'Durkheimians' who sought to establish the status of sociology as an academic discipline at the expense of the action-orientation of their mentor. This intellectual 'academic drift'[28] went alongside a drift in institutional ideology[29] and a celebration of detachment (as in Benda's *La trahison des clercs*, published in 1927).

The paper pays particular attention to the way in which Célestin Bouglé was instrumental in transforming Durkheim's sociology into academic philosophy. This provided a way-in to the fourth partisan dimension. I suggest that Bouglé influenced the intellectual development of Raymond Aron who, as professor of sociology at the Sorbonne, gave both Bourdieu and Passeron jobs in Paris when they returned from Algeria in 1960. Aron was already hostile to what he called Durkheim's 'sociologism' – his inclination to interpret everything, including politics, sociologically. Following Weber, Aron was intent on analysing political behaviour in its own right and equally intent on separating academic analysis from social engagement. By contrast, Bourdieu was committed to reviving the original action orientation of Durkheim's work. A rift between Bourdieu and Aron was effected by their different reactions to the student revolt of May 1968. By 1976, Bourdieu (with Boltanski) (Bourdieu and Boltanski, 1976) identified elements of the philosophical transformation of Durkheimianism of the 1930s as responsible for the counter-revolution which developed in France after the defeat of the student revolt. The paper extracts some references made by Bourdieu and Boltanski to language used in the 1930s which fed into post-1968 terminology and it singles out *Changer*, published by Jacques Delors in 1975. I use this to introduce consideration of whether the language of 'social exclusion' adopted by the European Union under the presidency of Delors was grounded in Durkheimian sociologism or was, instead, indicative of a managerialist conception of society which was fundamentally unsympathetic to grassroots communitarianism. The paper pursues this enquiry to examine the nature of the initiative introduced by Tony Blair in 1997, again making the suggestion, already apparent in the concluding paragraph of Chapter 4B, that Blair's social policy was driven by idealist morality more than by any sociologically aware commitment to enabling the participatory interaction of all citizens.

---

28. I used this phrase, coined by Pratt and Burgess to describe the gradual academicisation of the polytechnics, deliberately to suggest a parallel between the historical French situation and the recent English one.

29. As early as 1995 I had reviewed Charle and Verger's *Histoire des universités* and recognised that their social historical analysis contrasted with English history of universities, such as that published by Hastings Rashdall, which were auto-confirmations of idealist philosophy (see Robbins, 1995a).

This paper marks the culmination of the train of thinking which had led me to suppose that Bourdieu's commitment to promoting the life chances of disadvantaged people was based on a *sociological* theory which was located in progression from Durkheim. The paper starts and ends with commentary on Pierre Rosanvallon's *Le modèle politique français*. Rosanvallon was an 'Aronist' and there seemed to me to be a clear distinction between two approaches to the achievement of social justice. The Aronist solution deployed sociological analysis to manage society from a position of detached hauteur. The position represented by Bourdieu sought to achieve social harmony through the mutual understanding of civilians recognising each other as equals. The Bourdieusian solution which I supported involved sociological analysis but, importantly, he advocated an inclusive sociological orientation. Following the presentation of this paper I began to grapple with the problem that Bourdieu's sociology was grounded in philosophy without actually becoming identified academically with either sociology or philosophy. He advocated a form of socialism without supporting state socialism and, to that extent, he agreed with Rosanvallon in rejecting 'jacobinism', but he resisted the managerial authority of the new 'nobility' of politicians and administrators as supported by the Aronists. In essence, it became gradually clear to me that he was seeking to actualise a social ontology. Following from this recognition, I saw my task to be that of fighting on two fronts – ensuring that Bourdieu's work did not suffer the philosophical deformation imposed by Durkheimians on the work of Durkheim while also ensuring that his sociological legacy would not be appropriated by 'state' sociologists.

B. The Text

Pierre Rosanvallon holds the chair of modern history and contemporary politics at the Collège de France, Paris. In 2004 he published *Le Modèle politique français*, subtitled 'La société civile contre le jacobinisme de 1789 à nos jours' (civil society against jacobinism from 1789 to the present). I want to begin by summarising and scrutinising Rosanvallon's account of French political history since the Revolution and I shall hope to end with a critical account of his thesis, seeing it as representative of a partisan political position of the end of the twentieth century.

Rosanvallon's contention is that there are two possible political histories of France. On the one hand, there is the position consolidated by de Tocqueville which identified a 'jacobin tradition' or jacobinism, meaning a tradition which has constantly asserted the dominance of the central state, emphasising the importance of a direct relationship between the citizen and the state. On the other hand, Rosanvallon argues, this dominant representation of reality was always challenged by an opposing position which emphasised the significance of 'corps intermédiaires', various forms of associations, parties or local groups which interposed themselves between the extremes which confronted each other on the jacobin model. Not only was the jacobin model challenged by opposition, it also modified itself during the nineteenth century as it adapted to social and political change. Rosanvallon's purpose is not to deny the existence of the 'illiberal' jacobin tradition but rather to re-situate it, viewing its adaptations to change.

Jacobinism entailed the outlawing of political associations, but from ideological points of view which were not identical and became confused. An ideology of 'direct democracy' denied in principle the need for functions of delegation or representation. An ideology of 'immediate democracy' accepted that the people might develop a collective will but refused to institutionalise procedures whereby this might occur. The first part of Rosanvallon's book is devoted to an analysis of the ideological tensions inherent in what, instead of jacobinism, he prefers to call 'utopian generality'. The second part considers the development of this dominant ideology through the nineteenth century. From the 1880s, it was the republicans rather than the liberals who made the biggest impact on the inherited ideology. In the third part of the book, Rosanvallon analyses the legislation of 1884 on syndicates and of 1901 on associations. The first of these formally abolished the position advanced by Le Chapelier in 1791. Rosanvallon claims that there were two main reasons for this explicit renunciation of the jacobin ideology. The first reason was that there was a growing middle-class fear of socialism and the consequent sense that the recognition of syndicates might contain this advance. He traces the origins of the 1884 legislation back to the strategy of Napoleon III, which was to encourage the capacity of syndicates to look after the social welfare concerns of workers precisely so as to try to ensure that no political alliance should develop between workers and republicans. In turn, after 1871, the republicans proceeded to introduce the 1884 legislation in order to legitimise syndicalism as a social, but not political, movement. The second reason given by Rosanvallon for the rejection of the jacobin model was that the intellectual revolution of the emergence of sociology provided the tools for an objective critique of the political processes established by the French revolutionaries. Rosanvallon implies that sociology was effective because it offered scientific ammunition for discrediting the jacobin ideology. He devotes a subsection of his book to what he calls 'La sociologie contre le jacobinisme' (sociology against jacobinism). He offers little detailed discussion of Durkheim. I want to examine this subsection in some detail before turning to the work of Durkheim of this period in order to consider whether Rosanvallon misses the point in failing to acknowledge that sociology was attempting a positive intervention

rather than just a critique. Durkheim was attempting a sociological appropriation of political discourse and, in doing so, was attempting to make sociological analysis, institutionalised in university education, a vehicle for the
construction of mechanisms necessary for the introduction of the 'immediate'
democratic version of jacobinism.

[...]

Rosanvallon quotes from Durkheim's 1890 review of Thomas Ferneuil's cen-
tennial book – *Les Principes de 1789 et la Science sociale* (1889) – to show that
Durkheim was in essential agreement with Ferneuil, arguing that the principles
of the Revolution were, in effect, examples of the Comtist category of metaphysical thought and should now be supplanted by political reconstruction
founded on positivist research. The existence of any social contract had been
disproved by the analysis of social facts. It was necessary now to recognise
that associative mechanisms are required to mediate between individuals and
the state. Rosanvallon argues that Durkheim was neither étatiste nor liber-
tarian, and he quotes the following passage from Durkheim's *Une révision de
l'idée socialiste* of 1899:

> What liberates individuals is not the suppression of central regula-
> tion, but its multiplication, as long as these multiple centres are co-
> ordinated and subordinated one to another. (Durkheim, 1899, quoted in
> Rosanvallon, 2004, 273[30])

My point so far, as I move away from Rosanvallon's account of French social
political history, is that Rosanvallon wilfully diminishes Durkheim's intention
or aspiration. He treats the works of the sociologists at the end of the nineteenth century as epiphenomena of an essentially political progression, rating
the contributions of sociological texts merely as instruments which registered
social changes and participated in effecting further changes in the political
sphere. Sociological analysis was politically determined. There is no sense, for
Rosanvallon, in which the emergent social science could be thought to have
challenged the domination of political discourse. He refuses to acknowledge
the autonomous scientificity of Durkheim's work. The key issue, however, is
one which is paralleled analogously in the recognition of recent commentators
on the work of Weber, particularly Richard Swedberg, that, between the first
publication of 'The Protestant Ethic and the 'Spirit' of Capitalism' in 1905

---

30. Note that this text does not feature in the Lukes bibliography. Durkheim's text was
    reproduced in Durkheim, *Textes*, 1975, vol. 3, p. 171, which was the edition of Durkheim
    edited by Viktor Karady in the *Le Sens commun* collection of Editions de Minuit under
    the general editorship of Pierre Bourdieu.

and the publication of the revised version of the essay published posthumously in 1920 in *Gesammelte Aufsätze zur Religionssoziologie*, Weber shifted from seeking to develop a 'Social Economics' to seeking, instead, to develop an 'Economic sociology'. In other words, analoguously, the force of Durkheim's achievement was not that he simply was identifying, as Rosanvallon would imply, a social dimension of the political but, rather, that he was struggling to establish a sociology of the political whereby the autonomy of politics would be diminished.

Willie Watts Miller's discussion of the appropriate translation of key phrases of Durkheim's Latin thesis on Montesquieu of 1893 is highly germane. Constrained, perhaps, by the presence of political philosophers on his examining jury, Durkheim chose to talk about *scientia politica* rather than *scientia socialis*, but it is clear that the thesis followed Comte's critique of Montesquieu and sought to transform the legacy of his political science into a sociology of politics. As Watts Miller concludes,

> My own suspicion is that he [Durkheim] had in mind other, greater issues, or, at the least, to create mischief – by challenging the very conception of political science in vogue at the time, and by taking possession of the name in the cause of the approach and methods of sociology. (Durkheim, 1997, 4).

Also germane and, of course, of particular relevance to this conference, is the text of Durkheim's French thesis, also of 1893, *De la division du travail social*; the differences between the preface to the first edition of that text of 1893 and the preface to the second edition of 1902; and, additionally, the relationship between Durkheim's developing thought in this context and in relation to the social function of education. This is not the place to try to unravel the complexity of the relationship of Durkheim's developing thought to the progress of socialism and syndicalism in the period, but I do want to suggest tentatively a broad thesis. In 1937, Harry Alpert wrote an article on 'France's First University Course in Sociology' in the *American Sociological Review* – introducing Durkheim's course given in 1887 in the Faculty of Letters of the University of Bordeaux (Alpert, 1937). Fifty years on, Alpert emphasised the importance of the historical context of that first course of lectures, seeing it as symptomatic of the French attempt to establish order in the decades following defeat in the Franco-Prussian War and the Paris Commune in 1871. He wrote:

> A secular democracy, then, was the ideal towards which the Republicans strove. It was to be achieved and maintained by a free, universal, compulsory and secular state educational system for which the famous Ferry Laws laid the foundation. But Jules Ferry and his fellow Republicans

realized that the problems of social and national solidarity and of moral reconstruction could never be solved merely by changing the administrative set-up of the schools. Far more essential was a reorganization of the *content* and *spirit* of education. (Alpert, 1937, 312)

More concretely, Alpert emphasised that Louis Liard, who had been appointed Directeur de l'Enseignement supérieur by Ferry in 1884, had previously taught in Bordeaux and had been responsible for the introduction of the course in social science there. Alpert contends that there was a homology between the social scientific content of the course of lectures and the formal function of those lectures, that the lectures implemented their content or, if you like, that the medium was the message. This view is confirmed by the emphasis of the first edition of *De la division du travail social* of 1893. We are all familiar with the way in which Durkheim introduced this first edition, indicating that his intention was to advance a positivist science of ethics in opposition to a priori moral philosophy. The scientific analysis of the diversity of moral facts would contribute to the construction of social solidarity both by the communication of findings and by the pedagogic transmission of a paradigmatic process of mutual ethical understanding amongst citizens. Hence mass education and functional higher education would help society to cope with the disintegration of organic solidarity and assist in the constitution of the kind of mechanical solidarity that had become necessary. The foundation of a new intellectual discipline was inextricably linked with the establishment of a new form of socially participative political order, as Durkheim made clear in the closing paragraph of the conclusion to the first edition:

> Because certain of our duties are no longer founded in the reality of things, a breakdown has resulted which will be repaired only in so far as a new discipline is established and consolidated. In short, our first duty is to make a moral code for ourselves. (Durkheim, 1964 [1933], 409)

Durkheim's thinking was linked to the agenda of the fin-de-siècle republicans. However, the preface to the first edition was replaced in the second edition of 1902 and in the subsequent editions of 1907, 1911 and 1926, by 'Quelques Remarques sur les Groupements professionnels' (some notes on occupational groups). Although the substance of the book remained unchanged, the new preface succeeded in shifting the emphasis of the text quite dramatically. Whereas the discussion contained within the first edition was thought itself to be instrumental, through the media of publication and educational transmission, in encouraging individuals to embark on a Kantian moral endeavour to construct a collective social ethic, the preface to the second edition focussed on the social function to be performed by corporations in effecting the transition from organic to mechanical social order. The second edition changed the status of the analysis offered in the book. The text now provided an account of objective social phenomena. It would be the actions of corporations within society which would transform social values rather more than the scientific analysis of those actions. The shift introduced by the new preface signalled a partial retreat from the optimism of the mid-1890s in two respects. In the first place, it signalled diminished optimism about the social function of the intellectual. In the second place, and relatedly, it signalled diminished confidence that a sociocracy produced by an educational encadrement inspired by dominant social scientific knowledge content would supplant the political structures of the state. It was a shift from an attempted post-Comtist appropriation of Rousseauism by means of positivist social science towards a rather more Saint-Simonian celebration of the social engineering potential of professional organisations. It seemed, in Rosanvallon's terms, to be a shift from an essentially jacobin position towards an anti-jacobin one which acknowledged the function of 'intermediary bodies'. However, the jacobin tendency remained. Syndicalism was to be subordinated to socialism. The function of associations of workers and managers was not to attend to the welfare of their own members, acting in a circumscribed way independently of a political state organisation which liberally tolerated and sponsored their existence, but instead to be the change-agents for a new political order, integrating divided labour, through dialogue, into a new form of managed society. The function of social scientific research and education was to reflect this change agency constructively back to the agents rather than to be more directly engaged in the process.

My argument is that the shift which I have described in respect of Durkheim's position between 1893 and 1902 corresponded with an institutional shift in French higher education. French universities in this period need the kind of analysis offered of German universities by Fritz Ringer in *The Decline of the German Mandarins. The German Academic Community, 1890 – 1933* (Ringer, 1969) and which he in part provided in his *Fields of Knowledge: French Academic Culture in Comparative Perspective, 1890-1920*. [...] In the period before World War I, there was clearly an ideological conflict between institutions which was symbolised by the opposition between Durkheim's Sorbonne and Bergson's Collège de France. I am suggesting that the context of Durkheim's intellectual production was subjected to what has more recently been labelled 'academic drift' in respect of the early ideological defaulting of the new polytechnics in the United Kingdom in the 1970s. T. N. Clark's *Prophets and Patrons* of 1973, subtitled *The French University and the Emergence of the Social Sciences*, analysed this process of academic institutionalisation, but he paid little attention to its consequences in respect of the relations between social science and political action. He demonstrated that, in 1914, 'the Durkheimians were the most completely institutionalized grouping of social scientists in France, and their success in this regard certainly eclipsed all others' (Clark, 1973, 98), but he did not fully explore the relationship between the auto-institutional-isation of what he calls 'clusters' of like-minded individuals and the developing identity and ideology of university institutions as such. In the 1890s, these two processes were mutually supportive but, after Durkheim's death, this became less true. Clark proceeded to outline the career trajectories of some of Durkheim's associates or disciples, but he did not try to analyse the impact of their institutional positions on both their representation of Durkheim's work after his death and on their own adaptation of the Durkheimian legacy in their publications.

There needs to be a major research project to analyse in detail the social and institutional conditions which shaped the post-mortem interpretation and dissemination of Durkheim's work. All I can do here this afternoon to advance my argument is make a few comments specifically about the mid-1920s. The key political event of the period in which several editions of the work of Durkheim were published was the election in May 1924 of the Cartel des gauches, bringing to power a trio of normaliens – Herriot, Painlevé and Blum. The government was short-lived, Herriot resigning in April 1925, and the Cartel collapsed with the return to power of Poincaré on 27 July 1926, but it had attempted to introduce radical reforms in direct opposition to the Bloc National which it had supplanted. As Roderick Kedward has summarised the programme which Herriot set out in the autumn of 1924,

Wartime pacifists accused of relations with the enemy [...] were to be amnestied; striking railway workers, sacked *en masse* in 1920, were to be reinstated; civil servants were given the right to unionize; Jaurès was elevated to the highest national status in the Panthéon; concessions to religious sensibilities in Alsace and Lorraine were to be withdrawn and the French embassy in the Vatican to be dismantled. (Kedward, 2005, 134)

In short, the Cartel was anti-clerical and pro-syndicalist. Although Albert Thibaudet's account of the government of the Cartel, published in 1927, established the notion that it was a 'République des Professeurs', emphasising that the three ministers were all about 50 years old and had been formed attitudinally by the Dreyfus affair, in respect of educational policy the Cartel did not preserve the legacy of the reforming pioneers of the third Republic, such as Jules Ferry. These reformers had introduced compulsory primary education and *écoles primaires supérieurs* with the ideological intention of founding social solidarity educationally, but they had not attempted to disband what Edmond Goblot, writing in 1925, called *La barrière et le niveau*, the separate place in the system for lycées which alone could provide access to higher education. Immediately after World War I, the movement called the *Compagnons de la nouvelle université* advocated the establishment of an *école unique* – that is to say an undivided or comprehensive schooling system. They also argued that the aim of making universities encyclopaedic should be abandoned. This coincided with the view, expressed by Léon Bérard, minister of education of the Bloc National government in 1922, that the faculties should avoid too much theoretical teaching 'expensive for the state and the need for which is not always evident' (quoted in Zeldin, 1980, 325). The Durkheimians had to juggle their attachment to their master's early vision of totalising, conceptual encadrement with the new socialist vision of inclusive social equality based on the provision of opportunity for all to acquire socially useful skills. This juggling had to take place in a context in which Alain (Émile Chartier) was vigorously recommending philosophically a reflective, idealist detachment from instrumental knowledge and in which, in 1927, the one-time Radical, Julien Benda, published *La Trahison des clercs*, castigating the mundane social and political engagement of intellectuals.

Just one example of the juggling is Célestin Bouglé's preface of 1924 to assembled texts of Durkheim of 1898, 1906 and 1911. The first of these was 'Représentations individuelles et représentations collectives', first published in the *Revue de Métaphysique et de Morale*; the second was a text entitled 'Détermination du fait moral', which records both some theses presented by Durkheim to the Société française de Philosophie and the subsequent discussion; and the third was a text given at an international Philosophy Congress and published, again, in the *Revue de Métaphysique et de Morale* entitled 'Jugements de valeur et jugements de réalité'. At no point, of course, was *Sociologie et philosophie* a title which Durkheim would have countenanced even though the pieces were presented in philosophical contexts. In his presentation of the 2002 edition of *Sociologie et philosophie*, Bruno Karsenti rightly points out that Durkheim had argued in the conclusion of *Les règles de la méthode sociologique* of 1895 that the constitution of scientific sociology made it 'independent of all philosophy' (introduction by Karsenti in Durkheim, 2002 [1924], vii). This was not an acceptance of the coexistence of sociology with philosophy, but a claim that sociology had superseded philosophy. Whereas Durkheim's behaviour in relation to established philosophical discourse may correctly be understood to have been strategic, and whereas Simiand, Mauss and Halbwachs proceeded to situate their work as social science, Bouglé's intentions were more ambiguous. Bouglé sought to rescue Durkheimian thought from interpretations which, mainly based on *Les règles de la méthode sociologique*, identified 'sociologisme' with materialism and narrow scientism, hoping in this way to 'sauvegarder les droits de l'esprit' (preface by Bouglé in Durkheim, 2002 [1924], lxviii). Karsenti associates these interpretations with texts of Fouillé and Parodi published in Durkheim's lifetime and also particularly with Brunschvicg's *Les progrès de la conscience européenne* which was published in 1927.

My argument therefore is that in seeking to emphasise the non-materiality of Durkheim's thought and to reconcile it with elements of Kantian transcendentalism, Bouglé not only sought to legitimate sociology philosophically but also placed Durkheimianism in alliance with the kind of thinking of Alain and Benda, which opposed the engagement of philosophy with social and political affairs.

It is no accident that Bouglé was a kind of mentor in the 1930s to the still young Raymond Aron, nor an accident that Aron's doctoral thesis was supervised by Brunschvicg. Bouglé commissioned Aron to write *La sociologie allemande contemporaine* which was published in 1933 after Aron had spent a period of three years lecturing and studying in Germany. In that text Aron distinguished between the 'encyclopaedic sociology' represented by the Comte/Durkheim tradition and the 'analytic sociology' which characterised much of the developing German tradition. He wrote:

> The sociology of Comte and Spencer had as its object the whole of human history and the totality of society. It was the crown and synthesis of the social sciences. Simultaneously historical and systematic, it determined laws and values, it made human being a part of nature. It was under this guise that sociology, imported from France and England, first became known and rejected in Germany. (Aron, 1981, 1, my translation)

Aron had immediately signalled three of his lasting *bêtes noires*: his rejection, first of all, of the sociological attempt to usurp the function of philosophical history in seeking to take the whole of human history as its object; his rejection, secondly, of the sociological attempt to impose systematic unity on the diversity of social processes; and, thirdly, his rejection of what lay behind these two forms of conceptual appropriation: what he took to be the false inclination to deny any distinction between human and natural behaviour, that is to say the false endeavour to place human history within a bio-genetic evolutionary process rather than to acknowledge human transcendence of nature. Aron spent the war years in London and became a commentator of political events, consolidating his philosophical orientation to suppose that reality is essentially political rather than social. It was only in 1955 that he sought selection for an academic career and was elected to the chair of sociology at the Sorbonne. In the following decade, he repeatedly announced his hostility to the Durkheimian intellectual tradition and to the practical corollary of that tradition which he took to be the assertion of the primacy of social action. For Aron, sociological knowledge might assist political decision-making, but it could not usurp constitutional and legislative processes or determine what should be the ends of human society. […] Aron had no sympathy for idealist detachment from social and political affairs, but his commitment was to a Weberian balance between science and politics which had no time for the possibility that social science might immanently coincide with social action and stimulate social movements which might undermine political domination, or, more accurately, might insist on the redundancy of an independent sphere of political action.

Retrospectively, it is ironic that at the beginning of the 1960s Aron appointed Jean-Claude Passeron to be his research assistant at the Sorbonne and Pierre Bourdieu to be the secretary of his newly established research group. […] We know from Bourdieu's posthumously published *Esquisse pour une auto-analyse* (Bourdieu, 2004) that he had a sense of filial commitment to his father's attachment to the political vision of Jean Jaurès. During the 1970s Bourdieu began a series of studies which sought to demonstrate the dangers associated with attributing autonomous validity to the political sphere. 'L'opinion publique n'existe pas' of 1971 (Bourdieu, 1971) can be interpreted as an attack on the ways in which opinion polls appropriate sociological analysis to manufacture political evidence which eliminates genuine responsiveness to the diversity of social attitudes. The target here was the political exploitation of the kind of political science produced in the Sciences-Po in Paris. I want to focus briefly on an article which Bourdieu wrote with Luc Boltanski in 1976 entitled 'La production de l'idéologie dominante' in which, as the title suggests, they tried to show sociologically that the dominant political discourse in contemporary France was the product of a dominant social elite. It is significant that this article was written at about the same time as Bourdieu was analysing the way in which Heidegger had exploited everyday language to construct a 'pure' philosophical discourse which endorsed fascist political domination in his 'L'ontologie politique de Martin Heidegger' (Bourdieu, 1975). The linguistic approach is common to both articles and in both cases the authors argue that an insidiously partisan way of seeing the world linguistically becomes normalised through the operation of institutions which socially reproduce themselves. In this case, the target was, as Bourdieu and Boltanski put it, certain groups, notably Catholic intellectuals, who, 'since before the War, undertook to reconcile the irreconcilables of our time – the economy, religion, and science – by avoiding the equally abhorred alternatives of communism and radical-socialism'. (Bourdieu and Boltanski, 1976, 8). Bourdieu and Boltanski proceeded to narrow further their specification of these ideological culprits.

The search of these groups, they continued, 'for a third way [cette recherche d'une troisième voie] which often led to the threshold of fascism [...] anticipated down to the last detail the collective effort of the commissions of the Plan' (Bourdieu and Boltanski, 1976, 8). The ideological reconversion of the post-war period operationalised the debates of the pre-war period and those which took place during the war at Uriage which, they concluded, 'assured the continuity between the left of the Révolution nationale and the right of the Resistance' (Bourdieu and Boltanski, 1976, 8).

[...] As part of their article, Bourdieu and Boltanski attempted to produce an 'encyclopaedia of received ideas', seeking to demonstrate the way in which an ideology was constructed by the mutual citation of a limited number of authors, all engaged in a process of corporate legitimation through the publication of texts and participation in self-congratulatory conferences and meetings. The encyclopaedia was based on a reading of 35 books amongst which texts of Valéry Giscard d'Estaing and Michel Poniatowski feature prominently, but I want only to single out the attention given to the work of Jacques Delors. Bourdieu and Boltanski were attempting to delineate what we would now call the 'mantras' of an emergent dominant ideology.

Delors was born in 1925. He went to his local lycée and started employment at the Banque de France at the age of 19. He became a 'personalist', indebted to the thought of Mounier, in the 1950s and remained committed to personalism throughout his career. In 1957 the Banque de France released Delors to work on Tuesdays for the Confédération Française de Travailleurs Chrétiens (CFTC) and this brought him to the attention of Pierre Massé who was director at the Commisariat du Plan. Massé asked Delors to set up a social affairs department at the Commissariat and Delors began full-time work there in 1962. Meanwhile, during the Mollet government, Delors and Michel Rocard became the leading lights of the 'Second Left' movement which, during the Algerian War of Independence, rejected the Stalinism of the Communists and also the colonialist politics of the Radical Party. The Club Jean Moulin was one of the most influential clubs of the Second Left and Delors frequented the club. Delors supported Mitterrand's unsuccessful candidacy for the presidency in 1965, but in 1969 he became advisor on social affairs to Pompidou's prime minister – Jacques Chaban-Delmas. Delors remained in that post until Pompidou sacked Chaban-Delmas in 1972. He delayed two years before joining the Socialist Party in 1974. After Mitterrand's narrow defeat in the presidential election of 1974, Delors became fully committed to Mitterrand's team and became his leader on 'international economics' in 1976.

I give you these potted details of Delors's career to indicate that, at the date of Bourdieu and Boltanski's article in 1976, Delors's stance was typical of those which were the objects of the article's attempted exposé. Delors was a Catholic and, more specifically, a personalist. He had served in a Gaullist ministry but had become associated with Mitterrand's political fortunes, exhibiting an 'end of ideology' willingness to associate with whoever held power. In the light of this I want to revert to some of the quotations given by Bourdieu and Boltanski to illustrate some of the characteristics of the ideology which was insidiously becoming dominant. They provide some quotations under the heading of 'changement' in order to suggest that the new ideology implies support for the antithesis of revolution, the encouragement of unprincipled pragmatism. An extract is taken from Delors's book of 1975 entitled *Changer*. Delors is cited as saying that 'I attach a great deal of importance to change strategies and not simply to the definition of goals' (Bourdieu and Boltanski, 1976, 14). Bourdieu and Boltanski imply by association that this is the essence of the philosophy of the commissariat au Plan when they quote from a publication of the Club Moulin to the effect that 'Planning replaces regulation' ('Le plan remplace la règle') (Bourdieu and Boltanski, 1976, 28). Again, Bourdieu and Boltanski suggest that the new ideology is essentially managerial and anti-egalitarian. They quote from Bloch-Laine's *Pour une réforme de l'entreprise* of 1963 his comment that 'in every business, as in the whole of human society, there are the governed and the governors' (Bourdieu and Boltanski, 1976, 14) and, for our purposes today, this suggested orientation is reinforced by a quotation from Pierre Massé which features under the heading of 'Exclus'. An extract is given from Massé's *Le Plan ou l'anti-hasard* of 1965 in which he is presented as perceiving social exclusion in terms of threat: 'There is a risk that we shall see the emergence of what Mendras calls a counter-society, made up of those who don't want or can't conform [suivre la cadence]' (Bourdieu and Boltanski, 1976, 19), and this is cross-referred to entries under the headings of 'hippies' and 'May 1968' to illustrate this further. Under the heading of 'Elites', defined as the antithesis of the 'masses', Michel Poniatowski is quoted as saying in his book of 1972, *Cartes sur table*, that 'it is obvious that the world evolves thanks to elites. [...] Every evolution is achieved by a small number of especially gifted people' (Bourdieu and Boltanski, 1976, 17) and this cross-refers to entries on 'leaders' which is a deliberate recall of the emphasis of the ethos of Uriage. One final indicative entry is under the heading of 'Pauvreté' where the following extract from a 1961 text published by the Club Jean Moulin entitled *L'Etat et le citoyen* is quoted, saying, 'Poor people should have nothing to fear from a society where they have their place, from a society which understands them, which includes them', and this passage is cross-referred to the entries under 'Exclus'.

I have deliberately selected words related to poverty, inclusion and exclusion to give a particular emphasis to the way in which Bourdieu and Boltanski sought to identify a terminological nexus underlying the stances of a group of politicians largely associated with the Second Left. After Mitterrand's defeat in 1978, Delors supported Mitterrand in his resistance to Rocard's leadership challenge. Chévènement was rewarded for his comparable support by being given the opportunity to rewrite the party programme. The Socialist Party adopted this programme, called the 'Projet Socialiste', in 1980. Although Delors voted against this programme and spent a brief period in 1979 as a Member of the European Parliament, he was brought back to be minister of finance when eventually Mitterrand was elected president in 1981. Delors was, therefore, a member of the French socialist government which, in December 1981, failed to condemn the suppression of the Solidarity movement in Poland by General Jaruzelski. In his biography of Michel Foucault, Didier Eribon devotes a chapter to the reaction to this event in Paris which was the only moment ever of collaboration between Foucault and Bourdieu. They were both signatories to a statement which was published in *Libération* on 15 December 1981, which condemned the weakness of the government, likening its inaction to that of the socialist governments of 1936 and 1956 in relation to Spain and Hungary. At the same time, as Eribon puts it; 'Foucault also agreed with Bourdieu that they should contact the trade union CFDT (Confédération des Travailleurs Démocratiques). They hoped to develop ties between a workers' union and the intellectuals similar to those that had existed in Poland between Solidarity and the cultural and university milieus' (Eribon, 1992, 298). A week later, Bourdieu explained his position in an interview with Eribon entitled 'Retrouver la tradition libertaire de la gauche'. Asked why he had encouraged a liaison between intellectuals and trades unions, Bourdieu replied:

> Solidarity is a great non-military workers' movement which has been crushed by military force; and also a movement raised against State socialism. The power to think about society, to change society, cannot be delegated, certainly not to a State which gives itself the right to offer welfare to its citizens without them, not to say in spite of them. (Bourdieu (1981) cited in Bourdieu, 2002a, 167)

It might be said that this marks a decisive break in Bourdieu's thinking, away from attempts to transform society on the basis of his sociological analyses of educational practices towards active engagement with the syndicalist movement, understood broadly as a social movement. In other words, this represented a break which was comparable to the break I have tried to describe in Durkheim's thinking between the first and second editions of *De la division du travail social*.

After three years as minister of finance, Delors made it known that he would like the post of president of the European Commission and he was duly elected, commencing in January 1985. [...]

Delors's first goal was to achieve an European single market by 1992, but as early as 1988 Delors began to worry that, as his biographer Charles Grant puts it, 'the 1992 programme was turning the Community into a mere cornucopia for capitalists' (Grant, 1994, 83). As a result, Delors promised a series of Labour laws, to be inspired by a Social Charter, designed to achieve social integration. Grant quotes from a television interview which Delors gave in October 1987 to demonstrate how far Delors's social thought was still inspired by Christian personalism. Delors said:

> The individual must be able to fulfil himself, to be a real citizen, to be an active man in his work, but he also has obligations towards society. (Grant, 1994, 87)

The Social Charter was published in May 1989 and approved by all the 12 member states except the United Kingdom in December 1989 at the Strasbourg Council. The Action Programme which followed resulted in some 47 different instruments submitted to the Council by January 1993 (Endo, 1999, 107). The UK government was in denial about the existence of poverty in the United Kingdom, 'social exclusion' was thought to be an alien piece of eurospeak and the involvement of the Commission in social issues was thought to be part of a French-dominated attempt to mould Europe into a socialist, republican superstate. The assumption was that the concept of 'social exclusion' was predicated on the concept of 'solidarity' and was, therefore, intrinsically Durkheimian. I have tried to suggest, on the contrary, that the social agenda initiated by Delors was one which was in accord with the Second Left thinking of the 1960s and which, in Bourdieu's thinking, manifested a spurious, governmentally managed social inclusion which was antagonistic to socialism. [...] An enormous amount has happened since Tony Blair gave his speech entitled 'Bringing Britain Together' in December 1997 at Stockwell Park School, South London, at which he launched the Social Exclusion Unit as 'one of the most important new initiatives of this administration', designed to achieve 'national renewal' meaning 'Britain re-built as one nation, in which each citizen is valued and has a stake; in which no-one is excluded from opportunity and the chance to develop their potential'. In the terms which I have been discussing, I suspect, as did Bourdieu in the late 1990s, that the inspiration for the discourse of social inclusion was personalist more than socialist and that the Third Way celebrated by Tony Blair and

Anthony Giddens had characteristics not unlike those exposed by Bourdieu and Boltanski in respect of the legacy of the post-war thought of the earlier adherents of Uriage. In the United Kingdom we still have a Cabinet Office Social Exclusion Taskforce implementing the Social Exclusion Action Plan of September 2006, and, in Europe, a decision of the European Parliament and of the Council of December 2001 established a community Action Programme to Combat Social Exclusion for a period of five years. My question is whether these initiatives have had the effect or have intended to have the effect of securing the kind of sociopolitical solidarity envisaged by Durkheim in *De la division du travail social.*

I did promise that my lecture would come full circle by returning to the work of Pierre Rosanvallon. When, in November 1995, Alain Juppé announced a proposed reform of the social security system, it is no surprise to find that Rosanvallon was one of the signatories to a petition produced in favour of the reform, whilst Pierre Bourdieu was to become the dominant figure-head of the movement which expressed itself in opposition in 'a call to intellectuals in support of the strikers' of 4 December 1995. 'La pétition réforme' expressed reservations about aspects of Juppé's proposals, but it mainly contended that they offered the opportunity for debate about the roles of parliament and social partners in decision-making on health and social care issues.

This was what 'la pétition Grève' feared, believing that the strike in opposition to Juppé's proposals would provide an occasion for the re-emphasis of the social constitution of the political and for a rejection of the continued imposition of de Gaulle's suppression of the socialist constitutional reforms introduced after World War II.

Rosanvallon marginalises the ideological contribution of Durkheim and the Durkheimians precisely because recognition of the historical significance of Durkheim in generating a 'social politics' would necessarily seem to contradict the anti-sociological methodology of a book published with the intention of polemically recommending a resurgence of a post-revolutionary, political definition of democracy. Rosanvallon is, after all, director of the Centre de recherches politiques Raymond Aron and his opposition to Durkheim by omission is Aronian.

I have tried to trace aspects of what, in my proposed title, I called the political transformation of Durkheimianism. I think it would have been more accurate to have called what I have described as, rather, an account of the political deformation of Durkheim's thought, partly effected by some Durkheimians. Although I have sympathy for Bourdieu's general position, this was not intended to be a partisan paper and I hope I have raised questions which we can pursue, notably about the nature of Durkheim's thought itself and his changes of position, the contribution of his followers in shaping his legacy across the period since his death, the relation in 'Durkheimian' thinking between syndicalism and socialism, and, finally, the relative status in 'Durkheimian' thinking between the spheres of social and political action and the boundaries of explanation between social and political science.

Chapter 6

BOURDIEU AND THE FIELD OF POLITICS [2018]

A. The Background

The ESRC grant to work on Passeron covered 60 per cent of my time. The grant was extended until December 2008, and further time allowance and funding was provided to enable the production of *Sociological Reasoning* for which I contributed a substantial introduction. There were several effects of this funding. Firstly, the time out consolidated my detachment from the university. Until 2002, I had felt that my thinking and my actions were all integrally related to the developing self-conception of the university. This sense had been most strong between 1970 and 1992 when my work had seemed to be inextricably associated with the political stance taken by the institution within the UK higher education system. It revived a little between 1997 and 2002 as my concept of 'social politics' seemed to correspond with some of the initiatives of the Blair government.[1] At first, my disquiet at Blair's ideology was that it was insufficiently sociological. I soon realised that the problem was that the government's orientation was managerial rather than sociologistic. I saw a similarity between the deformation in France of Durkheimian sociology and the determination in England of the Labour Party to disregard the traditions of the trade union movement. I sensed that a covert moral idealism was rejecting positivist empiricism and that sociology was only being used as an instrument in policymaking rather than as a basis for reconceptualising society. For the first time, I had, after 1997, become involved in my local Labour Party. This has continued although I became disillusioned by the Labour government's disinclination explicitly to challenge some of the basic structural inequalities in our society, such as the monarchy, the House of Lords or public schools.

---

1. The establishment, for instance, of mayors and local assemblies seemed to be an attempt to enable the political participation of people to become less dependent exclusively on representation by elected MPs.

My detachment from the values of the institution – which had encouraged me to become involved in local party politics – was reinforced by the second effect of my ESRC research funding. Several of my publications had been submitted to the first Research Assessment exercise in 1996. This had eased my acceptance in the School of Social Sciences after my career in the School for Independent Study. Gradually, however, the process of securing funding for research and of contributing to income generation for the university through the recognition of my research outputs began to dominate. My work on Bourdieu was submitted in the Research Assessment exercise of 2001. This emphasis of research, in increasing separation from teaching, persisted through the first decade of the century. Within UEL I taught an undergraduate course for several years for the Department of Sociology, but I was mainly involved with PhD students, both supervising individual projects and running training seminars for successive cohorts of students. This involvement with PhD students was an attempt to place my research activity alongside theirs rather than to offer instruction. My endeavour was to communicate that research should start from life problems identified by researchers rather than from supposed inadequacies in theories advanced within disciplines. This meant that I was trying to encourage a socio-historical reflexion on the generation of those theoretical solutions adopted by disciplines which, too often, were taken by researchers as the starting points of their enquiries.

In my own work I tried to pursue this argument in several contexts. The paper given at Oxford in 2008 is one example of how I used the context provided by the Centre for Durkheimian Studies to suggest the need to deconstruct 'Durkheimianism' in order to restore the historical meaning of Durkheim's research. I was not just intent on exploring the transformation of concepts over time but also on analysing the implications of the ways in which concepts developed in specific sociopolitical contexts transferred to others. This became, increasingly, a *political* interest. Essentially, I wanted to investigate the ways in which concepts developed within a secular, republican tradition (France) have been adapted or appropriated within a liberal, monarchist tradition (Britain). The preparation of a new book for Sage, following the publication of *Bourdieu and Culture*, was the second context in which I set about considering these ideas. I proposed a book on 'the internationalisation of French social theory' which would consider the works of five French intellectuals of the mid- to late- twentieth century in such a way as to expose the differences between their meanings in the contexts of their production and the meanings as they were translated and interpreted in the English field of reception. The completion of this book was delayed as a result of the Passeron project, but through the period from 2006 to 2010 I systematically read the works of Aron, Althusser, Foucault, Lyotard and Bourdieu in their French and

English contexts. Importantly, I wanted to focus on the context of reception within British society rather than linguistically within the English-speaking world. I did a lot of work on the sociopolitical backgrounds to the appearances of the texts in both countries but, sadly, there was not enough space to allow this contextualisation to be included in the final text when it was published in 2010 as *French Post-War Social Theory*, and this title is indicative of the way in which the book had lost its concentration on the process of the cross-national transmission of ideas.

My thoughts developed in other contexts in these years between 2006 and 2010, but the common factor was that I sought to analyse the social conditions of the production of both sociology and philosophy. I was trying to produce a socio-history of concept formation. This was a difficult task because it was deploying a philosophy of sociology to undertake a sociology of philosophy. In 2007, I gave a paper at the British Sociological Association (BSA) annual conference which began by pointing to the anomaly of presenting my interpretation of Bourdieu within a framework predefined institutionally as sociological.[2] Following the Passeron project, I was invited by him and J. -L. Fabiani to be a Directeur associé in the École des Hautes Études en Sciences Sociales (EHESS) in 2009–10. I chose to give seminars, in Paris and Marseille, which would examine comparatively epistemological developments in France and Britain at 50-year intervals – 1850, 1900, 1950 and 2000. I was only able to explore the first two historical periods[3] in October 2009 and April 2010, but, in May, with Tim Jenkins, I organised a seminar for ESRC, NCRM on 'The epistemology of the social sciences' which related to the later periods by concentrating on *Le métier de sociologue* by Bourdieu, Chamboredon and Passeron (1968).

I was asked to retire at the end of the semester in which my 65th birthday fell (January 2010). My research outputs in the previous few years had been submitted for the 2008 Research Assessment Exercise. My contribution to the UEL sociology submission was thought to have been significant in attracting research income to UEL and this helped me secure fractional contracts at UEL from February 2010 through to January 2014, when I retired fully. These fractional contracts provided some continuing institutional sponsorship and support but, essentially, I became an independent researcher from 2010 onwards. I was saved from self-indulgence primarily through my association with a group of research students meeting nationally which was partly initiated by one of my PhD students, Jenny Thatcher, and others who had

---

2. 'Conceptual Transfer in Social Science and Politics: An Examination of the Thinking of Pierre Bourdieu, 1985–1995'. – unpublished*.
3. The main published output from these seminars was Robbins (2011b).

attended the ESRC/NCRM workshop. They organised two preliminary workshops/conferences with BSA funding, held at the universities of Bristol[4] and East London.[5] I was a guest speaker in both. In both presentations I tried to clarify that, in my view, Bourdieu's work should not be used exclusively in research which is circumscribed by the disciplinary framework of 'sociology'. In the first I argued that Bourdieu's orientation oscillated between 'nominalism' and 'realism' and that it was, therefore, as a precondition for using his work, important to evaluate the conditions in which he generated his concepts as well as the realist situations in which he deployed them. In the second, I tried to illustrate this in respect of educational research, arguing that the sociology of education should be constantly vigilant with respect to the political conditions setting its agenda. In short, I tried to encourage research students to be sociologically reflexive in pursuing their projects.

The group was formally established as a study group of the BSA in 2012. As the initiators argued in a publication which they produced in 2016, the central aim of the group was to 'extend and consider the application of Bourdieusian social theory into contemporary research' (Thatcher et al., 2016, 1) and to achieve this by 'bringing together researchers from different areas of inquiry and stages of career to foster an academic community' (Thatcher et al., 2016, 1). There were several important characteristics. The first was that the group operated as a community which quickly grew in size and influence, operating internationally through its website. The second was that the members of the group were largely young researchers who were active in the post-1992 British universities. The consequence, on both counts, was that the group began to constitute an alternative, subversive movement which was as sympathetic to Bourdieu's late political activism as to his intellectual position. The study group was invaluable for me. It offered me, in retirement, membership of a community of young intellectuals in which I could discuss ideas and projects. Its ethos also confirmed my anti-academic orientation within sociology. During the period between 2012 and 2019, I was given the opportunity to share some of my developing ideas about Bourdieu's work. The group tried to maintain a balance between theory and practice and this encouraged me to try to interpret Bourdieu's position in this respect.

There were several key moments in my contributions to the Study Group workshops/conferences. At a 'Bourdieu and Public Sociology' workshop in

---

4. My paper was 'From Theory of Sociological Knowledge to Theory of Practice' – unpublished*.
5. My paper was 'Politics and the Sociology of Education' for a conference on *Social Class and Educational Aspiration* – unpublished*.

June 2012, I gave a paper entitled 'Political Interventions. Social Science and Political Action' in response to one given by Michael Burawoy. I tried to insist that Bourdieu's work should be understood socio-genetically rather than in theoretical abstraction. Increasingly I was interpreting the historicity which I had derived from Passeron in terms of an emphasis on the 'life-world' conditions of science. My introduction to *On Bourdieu, Education and Society* (2006) had been my first attempt to suggest that the production and reception of all texts should be analysed phenomenologically. In particular, I followed Bourdieu in his interest in the work of Husserl and Heidegger on time. This became apparent in a talk I gave at a Study Group conference in July 2016, entitled 'Bourdieu and Heidegger: Epistemology, ontology and the prospects for social science'. As the title suggests, I was beginning to understand Bourdieu as a social ontologist more than as a sociologist. The paper which follows, given at the second annual conference of the Study Group in July 2018, entitled 'Reproduction and Resistance', was an attempt to pursue this orientation in relation to the field of politics.

To introduce this paper more adequately, I need to say more about the progression of my publications which proceeded alongside the development of my ideas within the context of the Study Group. Before the publication of *French Post-War Social Theory*, I was invited to give a plenary lecture at a conference organised by the Department of Sociology of the University of Copenhagen.[6] I used the opportunity to reflect on the relationship between the thinking of Lyotard and Bourdieu as it had become apparent to me in working on the book. This was beginning to confirm my inclination to understand the phenomenological element in Bourdieu's work, especially in respect of political behaviour.[7] In 2012, I was given the chance to revise for a second edition the contribution which I had made in 2008 to *Pierre Bourdieu: Key Concepts* (Grenfell, 2008).[8] In my contribution to the first edition I had drawn on the reading which I had done for *French Post-War Social Theory*, this time in respect of the work of Althusser. I had emphasised that Bourdieu became increasingly aware of the danger that the theory of practice which he had outlined in his book of 1972[9] might become the basis of detached, theoreticist enquiry rather than an instrument for understanding social practices. In the 1990s, when Bourdieu became most politically 'active', his main concern became to ask, as Althusser put it in 1970, 'by what mechanism does the process of knowledge, which takes place entirely in thought, produce the cognitive appropriation

---

6. 'Beyond Bourdieu – Habitus, Capital & Social Stratification'.
7. The presentation was subsequently published, Robbins (2011c).
8. Robbins (2008).
9. Bourdieu (1972, 1977).

of its real object, which exists outside thought in the real world?' (Althusser and Balibar, 1970, 56, cited in Grenfell, 2008, 39). For my contribution to the second edition, I added several paragraphs[10] which indicate, through brief references to Alfred Schutz and Aron Gurwitsch, that I was now beginning to use their competing interpretations of Husserl as a means towards explicating the relationship between thought and action in Bourdieu's work. This was the prelude to the detailed treatment in *The Bourdieu Paradigm* (Robbins, 2019).

In publications of the following years, I pursued this issue of the relationship in practice between thought and action. Sage launched a new series – Sage Swifts – in which I published *Cultural Relativism and International Politics* (Robbins, 2014). Especially in my discussion of Raymond Aron's work, I used this book to examine the status of political *science* in relation to political journalism, concluding that, nationally and internationally, there is a need for political understanding to be based on cross-cultural recognition of difference rather than on a detached discourse of science. In the same year, I explored further the question of internationalism in a paper I was invited to give at a conference on 'Modernity: Culture Tradition and Morality Reconstruction' in the Institute for Advanced Study in European Culture, Shanghai Jiao Tong University, Shanghai.[11] I used an understanding of 'constitutive phenomenology' developed by Aron Gurwitsch[12] to show that Bourdieu's early analyses of traditional Algerian tribes had been pre-conceptualised by the colonial anthropological sources which he deployed and that he eventually tried to eliminate this conceptual imperialism by suggesting that cross-national exchanges should be fostered which are based on socio-analytic encounter and not on the superimposition of one dominant frame of thinking. I consolidated this argument when I was asked to edit the volume on Bourdieu in the Anthem Companions series. I invited contributors from diverse cultures to try to articulate the way in which Bourdieu's analyses, derived from his French situation, impinged on their indigenous understandings.[13]

In 2018, I was writing *The Bourdieu Paradigm* in which I juxtaposed Bourdieu's work with that of some disciples of Husserl, including Gurwitsch. I was exploring the relationship between Gurwitsch's 'field of consciousness' and Bourdieu's 'field' theory when I received an invitation to speak at the 2nd

10. Robbins, (2012, 39–40).
11. My paper was entitled 'Socio-analytic Encounter and International Relations: Cross-Cultural Conceptualisation of "Traditionalism" and "Modernity"'. See 2nd High-level International Academic Forum 'Modernization: China and the World', Shanghai Jiao Tong University, Proceedings, 86–99.
12. A. Gurwitsch, *The Collected Works of Aron Gurwitsch, 1901-1973, Volume 1. Constitutive Phenomenology in Historical Perspective*, ed. J. Garcia-Gomez, the Netherlands: Springer, 2009.
13. Robbins (2016).

biennial conference of the Bourdieu Study Group in July. The conference was entitled *Reproduction and Resistance*. It took place half way through Mrs May's term as prime minister – between the General Elections of 2017 and 2019. Support in the country for the Labour Party under Jeremy Corbyn was still strong and there was a strong sense that most of those attending the conference were his supporters. Implicitly, I raised the question whether 'Corbynism' was primarily a social movement and, therefore, the further question of what might be involved to adapt it successfully to the existing political system. To address this question indirectly, I discussed the development of Bourdieu's 'field' theory and, especially, the article in which he offered a discussion of the field of politics. The essence of what I was implying was that Bourdieu conceptualised the political field as one which is not stable and fixed but is one which is *formally* involved in continuously adapting the structured structures of its institutions in response to the structuring structures within society. The implication was that social movements should not *politicise* themselves in conformity with dominant political practices but should endeavour to transform those practices in accordance with their social aims. My theoretical argument was illustrated by reference to the by-election which had recently taken place in my own constituency. I suggested that the processes of the election and the electoral turnout showed that a self-fulfilling parliamentary system was out of touch with the population.

B. The Text

In the time available to me today, I want, first, to say something about the development of Bourdieu's thinking about politics and then, second, to say something about his various 'field' projects. I will then try to bring these two themes together by focussing on his 'La représentation politique. Éléments pour une théorie du champ politique' (1981) – translated as 'Political representation: Elements for a theory of the political field', in his *Language and Symbolic Power*, edited by J. Thompson (Cambridge: Polity Press, 1991, pp. 171–202), making some comparison with his treatment of the field of religion in 'La sainte famille: L'épiscopat français dans le champ du pouvoir' (1982) – untranslated, about the French episcopacy, which was co-authored with Monique de Saint Martin. I will suggest that Bourdieu *conceptualised* the field of politics in 'La représentation politique'. Published at almost the same time, 'La sainte famille' was a report on a research project on bishops and the French Church which provides hints about the way in which a comparable study might have been undertaken on French politicians and the political system. Finally, I will explore some possibilities for the practical deployment of Bourdieu's concepts and methods in relation to the political field by reference to the recent by-election which took place on June 14 in the constituency in which I live –Lewisham East.

First of all, therefore, we are I'm sure all familiar with the fact that Bourdieu's work was never a-political. Two posthumous publications remind us of this. Tassadit Yacine edited all of the minor texts which Bourdieu wrote in Algeria in *Esquisses algériennes* (2008), translated in 2013 as *Algerian Sketches*, and Franck Poupeau and Thierry Discepolo assembled in 2002 texts which Bourdieu had produced throughout his career as *Interventions, 1961–2001. Science sociale et action politique* which was published in translation in 2008 by Verso as *Political Intervention. Social Science and Political Action*. If we didn't already know, we found out from these publications a history of Bourdieu's political orientation. We know that, as a conscripted soldier in Algeria in 1956, he was already hostile to the French colonial presence that he was obliged to be involved in imposing. When he quickly managed to get himself transferred to an intelligence job, he proceeded to use the opportunity to write reports in which he outlined the implications of French colonial presence on traditional Algerian society. The important point, however, is that these were not strictly *political* analyses or *political* interventions. You only have to compare what Bourdieu wrote at this time with what Lyotard was writing at the same time when, based in Constantine in Algeria, he was the Algerian political correspondent for the journal *Socialisme ou Barbarie*. Lyotard's essays were subsequently collected and published in 1989 as *La guerre des algériens* and included in translation in 1993 in *Jean-François Lyotard: Political Writings*. Lyotard reported in detail on the disputes and machinations within the Algerian revolutionary movement, all in the context of a debate about the stance of the Communist Party in respect of colonialism. By contrast, Bourdieu analysed French political intervention in Algeria as only one dimension of the total imposition of Western culture on traditional cultural and social organisation. Towards the end of the Algerian War of Independence, he wrote 'Révolution dans la révolution' (revolution within the revolution) (1961) in which it was clear that he feared that independence would only gain power for an indigenous elite in place of the domination of the French administration. At the end of *Le déracinement* (The Uprooting), which was not published in France until 1964, he tried to argue that the establishment of a comprehensive educational system in the newly independent state of Algeria could be the process which would ensure that independence was for the whole people rather than for an urban elite.

That, of course, relates to the findings of the educational research undertaken by Bourdieu and Passeron in France in the early 1960s also published in 1964 as *Les héritiers* (The Inheritors) in which they showed that the French educational system reinforced the privilege of the culturally advantaged. The main point is that Bourdieu was searching for social transformation.

During the May events of 1968, the student revolt, Bourdieu argued that the reform of the educational system that was needed should not be pursued on the basis of the demands of students who were already the beneficiaries of the flawed system. He called vainly for a new Estates General, reviving the Estates General of the early days of the French Revolution in 1789, so as to initiate an inclusive debate. This was the basis of his disagreement with his mentor, Raymond Aron, who argued that the student revolt was an unrealisable revolution, recommending instead that bureaucratic reforms should be introduced by the Gaullist government from the top down. Bourdieu thought that a social revolution was the necessary prerequisite for political revolution. It was after the failure of the May events that Bourdieu began to conceptualise his politics as a counter-political social movement. One of the early indications of his post-1968 political position is the paper which he gave at a conference in January 1971, which was subsequently published in 1973 in *Les Temps Modernes* as 'L'opinion publique n'existe pas' (public opinion does not exist). This was the time when he was writing *Esquisse d'une théorie de la pratique*, 1972, (*Outline of a Theory of Practice*, 1977) in which he was beginning to articulate his post-structuralist methodology, distinguishing between the primary, experiential knowledge of situations and that of socially and intellectually detached scientists. The epistemological argument of that book was put into practice in 'public opinion does not exist' in an analysis of the way in which pollsters manufacture a 'public opinion' by systematically eliminating the opinions of those who are not equipped to answer the questions as they are posed. Pollsters ignore 'no responses', ignore the valid ways in which people might conceptualize their own experiences, in the same way as administrators had been disinclined to consult the real will of the people during the student revolt of 1968.

What we have, therefore, is Bourdieu arguing that political discourse is exclusive and is designed to sustain the power of those already initiated into that discourse. Just as in *The Inheritors* it was unclear what solution Bourdieu was proposing, so here. In both cases, the solution can go in one of two ways. Either the real public is enabled by education to participate in the dominant discourse such that it no longer is a discourse of domination, or the whole society, the dominated and the dominant, should, in equal socio-analytic encounter, construct a common discourse in which neither is privileged and in which, eventually, discourses are homogenised.

By the end of the 1970s there was, for Bourdieu, a new factor. He was appointed, in 1981, to the chair of Sociology at the Collège de France, which gave him a position of power and authority. Implicitly he discussed the implications of this in his 'Les trois états du capital culturel' (the three states of cultural capital) in which he refined his original position in respect of 'cultural capital'. He argued that the three states are of 'incorporated capital', 'objectivated capital' and 'instituted capital'. To put this in his personal terms, he was suggesting that he possessed capital which derived from his primary experience but which was additionally sustained and modified by the recognised status of his publications and, now, by the authority bestowed on him by the institution within which he worked. In other words, Bourdieu now accepted that the sociopolitical situation is not one of absolute confrontation between dominated and dominant but that primary opinions can be articulated through instituted media. Bourdieu articulated this modification of his earlier view in the chapter of *Distinction* devoted to 'Culture and Politics' which can be seen to be a revisiting of 'L'opinion publique n'existe pas' which recognises that the views of the dispossessed can be expressed through social organisations or political parties.

This is the background to the publication which I want to look at in more detail shortly: 'Political representation', which was published in 1981. The attitude which Bourdieu had adopted towards political pollsters is now directed at politicians themselves. The questions now are: how do politicians represent the public which elects them and what is the function in that process of political parties and political discourse? Before I move towards discussing this article, however, I want to sketch the parallel development of Bourdieu's theory of 'fields' and his empirical use of that theory.

Bourdieu's first use of the term 'champ' (field) was in the article which he contributed in 1966 to a special number of *Les Temps Modernes* devoted to the problems of structuralism: 'Champ intellectuel et projet créateur' (intellectual field and creative project). There he argued that 'intellectuals', which might include scientists as well as artists, liberated themselves during the nineteenth century such that their production was no longer dictated by either the Church or the Aristocracy. An 'intellectual' field became autonomous, establishing its own rules of legitimacy and enabling critical exchange within these shared rules. This was a liberation from clerical or aristocratic censure, but Bourdieu was aware that it might be at the expense of authentic expression of social origins. Autonomy generated 'art for art's sake' and, equally, 'science for science's sake', both of which excluded the public which was not initiated into the rules of their practice. By the early 1970s, alongside the development of the three forms of knowledge, Bourdieu became particularly interested in the behaviour of different kinds of fields, no longer supposing that it was meaningful to talk simply about an 'intellectual' field. He used the three forms of knowledge framework to suggest that different fields have their own rules. These are their 'structured structures', as he outlined in 'Sur le pouvoir symbolique' (first given in 1973 and published in 1977) (On Symbolic Power, 1991), but these are all subject to scrutiny in terms of the social conditions which produced them, their 'structuring structures' as he called them in the same article.

In 1976, Bourdieu gave a paper entitled 'Quelques propriétés des champs' (some properties of fields) at the École normale supérieure to a group of philologists and historians of literature. The paper was first published in Bourdieu (1980) (2nd edition, 1984). Here he clarified that 'there are *general laws of fields*' such that, for instance, the fields of politics, philosophy and religion have 'functionally invariant laws' and such that, additionally, every study of any specific field contributes to an understanding of the 'universal mechanisms of fields' (Bourdieu, 1984, 113; 1993b, 72). Fundamentally, every field is the locus of a struggle between those in possession of authority who seek to conserve that authority by maintaining an orthodoxy and those possessing less capital who seek to subvert existing authority by courting heresy or heterodoxy. Nevertheless, both conservers and subversives maintain the structure of the field which Bourdieu defines as 'a *state* of power relations between the agents or institutions engaged in the struggle' (Bourdieu, 1984, 114; 1993b, 72), that is to say not a static, substantive state but rather one which is held in existence by continuous conflict. Bourdieu's interest in 'field' theory was twofold. He sought to analyse the internal mechanisms of a range of fields but, given that they are all sub-fields of the social system, he became increasingly preoccupied with the relations between fields and with the ways in which actors deploy those relations to maximise their positions within the social system.

Just to summarise, here, chronologically, are most of the important articles, relating to 'fields', which Bourdieu published in the following years. I need to do this because quite a few of the articles remain untranslated and are relatively unknown:

'Champ du pouvoir, champ intellectuel et habitus de classe' (1971) [field of power, intellectual field, and class habitus] – untranslated, on the literary field.

'Le champ scientifique' (1975) – a different version of which was translated as: 'The specificity of the scientific field and the social conditions of the progress of reason' (1975)

'Anatomie du goût' (1976) – untranslated, on the field of taste. This fed into *La Distinction* (1979) which itself can be regarded as an analysis of the field of taste.

'le patronat' (1978) – untranslated and about French business leaders. Much of it reproduced in *La noblesse d'état* (1989), translated as *State Nobility*, 1996, Cambridge, Polity.

'La représentation politique' (1981) which I've already mentioned.

'La sainte famille' (1982) which I've already mentioned.

Homo Academicus (1984) can be regarded as an analysis of the academic field.

'La force du droit. Éléments pour une sociologie du champ juridique' (1986) – translated as 'The Force of Law: Toward a Sociology of the Juridical Field' (1987).

'Le champ littéraire' [the literary field] (1991) – a modified version is in *Les règles de l'art* (1992) [*The Rules of Art*, 1996].

'Le champ économique' [the economic field] (1997) – a modified version is in *Les structures sociales de l'économie* (2000) [*The Social Structures of the Economy* (2005)]

It must always be remembered as well that Bourdieu's personal work occurred within a collective context. The work by Alain Darbel and Dominique Schnapper, *Les Agents du système administratif* (The Agents of the Administrative System), Paris-The Hague, Mouton, 1969, is an example of an analysis of civil servants and the field of administration which complemented the other field researches being undertaken within the Centre de Sociologie Européenne.

These articles were of a mixed nature. Some, such as the analysis of the field of law, were what I would call scoping exercises, discussing theoretically what might be the particular characteristics of the field in question. Some, such as the article on business leaders and the one on French bishops, presented the findings of empirical research, analysing the characteristics of people holding power within their respective fields. In terms of the title of this conference, we can say that Bourdieu was exploring the mechanisms of reproduction in different fields. In other words, it is important to recognise that the concept of 'reproduction' is not just related to the field of education. The book of 1970 entitled *La reproduction* has been taken primarily to be a contribution to the sociology of education but, in fact, it was an initial investigation of the mechanisms operating within one field which Bourdieu then extended to many other fields.

I want to turn quickly to 'Political Representation'. I suggest that this is a scoping exercise which considers the nature of the field of politics, but I want to argue that this is capable of being reinforced empirically in the way in which Bourdieu and Monique de Saint Martin examined the field of the French episcopacy. 'Political Representation' has 10 subsections which overlap slightly. In his introduction, Bourdieu argues that the 'political field' has no intrinsic necessity. Its structure is determined at any time by the differential distance between the represented and the representatives. In other words, he implies that the current structure can be socially deconstructed and socially reconstructed. He then discusses 'The Monopoly of the Professionals', that is, that political power is in the hands of a professional elite. Again, he argues that this is a relative rather than absolute situation: the concentration of power in professionals is higher where the population lacks time or capital to participate. He argues that instituted political parties depend on influence delegated by the culturally impotent. Abstention is the only way to escape the mind-control of the professional politicians. Next Bourdieu has a section on 'Competence, stakes, and specific interests' in which he argues that the kind of political 'competence' communicated in 'political science' at Sciences-Po in Paris perpetuates a discourse which is an instrument of exclusion. The attack which he had originally made against opinion pollsters is now directed at the language internally sustained within the structured structure of political discourse which is designed to keep the structuring structure of society in general in subordination. Importantly, Bourdieu then describes the nature of 'the double game' played by politicians, on the one hand, representing the views of the people who elect them and, on the other hand, position-taking within their party and within parliament. He sees this as an inevitable problem: that of the bureaucratisation of revolution. Bourdieu next analyses 'slogans and mobilizing ideas' and he here suggests that the mobilisation effected by politicians is increasingly subordinated to the appropriated mobilisation undertaken by media commentators. This relates to the points Bourdieu was later to make in *On Television* about the corrupting effects of media. Next Bourdieu considers what he calls 'credit and credence'. This is about the ways in which politicians construct their public identities, either by cultivating local contacts to become known as a 'good local MP' or by performances in parliament or, again, increasingly, by performance on chat shows. This is related to the kinds of political capital MPs possess or attempt to acquire, either 'personal' capital, or 'delegated authority' obtained in succession to a previous post-holder or by dependence on the support of the party apparatus. The two concluding sections are important. The first is called 'the institutionalization of political capital'. Bourdieu describes the process whereby the maintenance of the political apparatus becomes more important than the realisation of its original goals. Because of this process, he comments:

It is thus easy to understand how political parties can be brought in this way to sacrifice their programmes so as to keep themselves in power or simply in existence. (Boudieu, *Language and Symbolic Power*, ed. J. Thompson, 1991, 197)

It is clear from this section that Bourdieu was acknowledging that the political field is incapable of satisfying the needs of the social with the result that his engagement of the 1990s was in support of social movements which he conceived as 'counter-political' rather than replacement or substitute politics. Fundamentally, he regarded the political system as not fit for purpose in respect of his social vision.

That was a quick summary of an article which, I hope you can see, resonates with many of our contemporary problems. As I've said, this was a kind of scoping exercise in respect of the field of politics. I want to indicate by quick reference to 'La sainte famille' the way in which it would be possible to subject politicians to analysis in the way in which bishops were in that project. I will then make a few comments about the political situation in Lewisham East, before finishing by discussing some of the possibilities for resistance which follow from Bourdieu's thinking.

'La sainte famille' was based on analysis of data primarily about the French episcopacy in 1972 in such a way as to generate comparison with the contemporary 'field' projects which were looking at the situations of business directors, professors and civil servants. The research extracted details of the social backgrounds, career trajectories and positions of ecclesiastical power of all the bishops in mainland France at that date, and the information gathered was complemented by in-depth interviews with 15 bishops. The article is devoted to an analysis of the processes by which mind-controlling power is acquired. Bourdieu is not offering a secular critique of theological or ecclesiastical claims but is providing what he thinks is a generalisable case study of power acquisition and imposition. One key component of the internal struggle within the Church which, nevertheless, the institution contrives to conceal in order to present itself homogeneously to the population is an opposition in recruitment between 'oblates' and inheritors. Bourdieu suggests that there is an opposition between the 'oblates' who, 'devoted to the Church since early infancy, invest totally in an institution to which they owe everything' and the inheritors who, ordained relatively late in life, are already in possession of cultural capital acquired in other fields. In a footnote, Bourdieu adds that 'the same law which apportions devotion and attachment with respect to an institution relative to dependency and indebtedness towards it also governs the relations which agents have with universities, trade unions and political parties'.

I am suggesting that one consequence of Bourdieu's field studies, therefore, is that we should undertake an empirical analysis of political representation. I will try to indicate the contemporary relevance of this in the United Kingdom in bourdieusian terms in a few comments on Lewisham East. I haven't had time to do a detailed analysis, but here are the outlines of an argument.

The borough of Lewisham has three parliamentary constituencies: Lewisham Deptford, Lewisham West and Penge, and Lewisham East. According to the Lewisham Joint Strategic Needs Assessment and based on projections of 2011 of the Greater London Authority, Lewisham is the 15th most ethnically diverse local authority in England, and two out of every five residents are from a Black and minority ethnic background. The largest Black, Asian and minority ethnic (BAME) groups are Black African and Black Caribbean: Black ethnic groups are estimated to comprise 30 per cent of the total population of Lewisham. In 2008/9 there were 35,062 pupils enrolled in Lewisham's 91 schools, 61 per cent of which were from BAME communities. This percentage of BAME pupils is significantly different from the proportion within the resident population. This could be interpreted as an indication of the future ethnic make-up of Lewisham's adult population. I don't have figures for the Lewisham East constituency but the profile of the borough is indicative.

From 1979 to 1997 the constituency was a marginal seat. Since the 1997 General Election the seat has swung towards Labour. Heidi Alexander was elected in May 2010. There was a turnout of 63.3 per cent of a registered electorate of 65,926. Her majority was 6,216. She is a white person. Educated at a comprehensive school in Swindon, she read Geography at the University of Durham and then gained a master's degree in European Urban and Regional Change. She was a researcher for MP Joan Ruddock for six years from 1999. She was elected as a Councillor in a Lewisham ward in 2004 and became deputy mayor in 2006. In the General Election of May 2015, her majority was 12,333. There was a turnout of 64.1 per cent of a registered electorate of 66,913. In September 2015, she became Shadow Secretary of State for Health in Jeremy Corbyn's shadow cabinet. In the European referendum of June 2016, I only have the breakdown for the whole of Lewisham. There was a turnout of 63.1 per cent of an electorate of 197,514. A total of 64.6 per cent voted to remain and 35.4 per cent voted to leave. Three days after the European referendum, she resigned from the shadow cabinet. In the General Election of June 2017, she increased her majority. It became a 21,123 majority. There was a turnout of 69.3 per cent of a registered electorate of 68,124. As it happens, there were Council elections in Lewisham on 3 May 2018. A 100 per cent Labour council was elected. In the seven wards constituting Lewisham East, the average turnout was 37.3 per cent. No Labour candidate gained less than 15 per cent of the total vote and one councillor, Janet Daby, gained 26 per cent of the vote in her ward. She was made deputy mayor. On May 8, Heidi Alexander announced that she was resigning as MP to take a job as a deputy mayor of London under Sadiq Khan. The Labour National Executive invited applications to succeed her. The National Executive drew up a shortlist from the long list and, at very short notice, invited constituency members to attend a meeting in central London to make their views known of the shortlisted candidates. The local party successfully insisted that there should be a local hustings. The National Executive Committee (NEC) selected four BAME women as potential candidates. One withdrew before the hustings. At the hustings, the three candidates gave short presentations, answered questions and a vote followed. The three candidates were the recently appointed deputy mayor, one candidate backed by Momentum and another candidate backed by Unite. In their presentations, the first candidate mentioned that she had studied at the LSE and had gained a master's degree, and also mentioned that she had been instrumental in establishing a local food bank and in supporting protests of firefighters against cuts. The Momentum-backed candidate mentioned that she was a lawyer but did not detail her qualifications. She emphasised that the constituency needed to engage more of its population in political activity. The third candidate did not mention her education but emphasised her union experience. The deputy mayor, Janet Daby, was selected as the candidate with a substantial majority out of about 450 people, followed by the Momentum-backed candidate with the Unite-backed candidate coming last. I was at the meeting and my guess would be that about 90 per cent of those present were white. At the by-election which was held on 14 June 2018, Janet Daby retained the seat for Labour with a majority of 5,629. The turnout was 33.3 per cent of a registered electorate of 66,140. Janet Daby gained 50.2 per cent of the votes cast but I have been emphasising the turnout figures to show that she received 11,033 votes which constitutes about 16 per cent of the electorate.

I hope this has not been too detailed. In terms of Bourdieu's thinking about the field of politics, I am wanting to emphasise that the turnout figures show that many of the electorate throughout were 'no response' electors, that is to say, no voters or abstainers. I have not been able to correlate no voters with BAME communities, but this seems likely. If you read Derron Wallace's contribution to *Bourdieu: The Next Generation*, 2016, you will see from his analysis of schooling in Lewisham ('south London') that he follows Bourdieu in identifying that the cultures of BAME students are not accommodated within the schooling system. I think it is likely that analysis of the voting figures would suggest that, even when the NEC imposes a BAME candidate, little progress has been made in generating representation of the interests and values of the non-voting population. This suggests that minority groups within the United Kingdom remain supplicant groups which are effectively excluded from the games of politics played by professional politicians.

Black MPs are caught in what Bourdieu regarded as the 'double game' of politics – representing those who elect them and position-taking within parliamentary debate. The social challenge which Bourdieu posed is to find ways to involve the whole population in decision-taking about its future. I think Bourdieu contemplated three kinds of resistance. The first is the solution which he implemented in the 1990s which is apparent from his 'Firing Back', anti-neoliberal publications. He tried to mobilise a counter-political social movement. He elaborated on this process in a booklet entitled *Les usages sociaux de la science* (1997) (The Social Uses of Science) in which he offered a blue-print for how staff in a scientific institute might gain control of the research agenda of their institute. The second solution is the one which he adopted in most of his career, and which he outlined theoretically in an article published at about the same time as 'Political Representation' and also published in translation in *Language and Symbolic Power*: 'Description and Prescription'. This solution involves analysing the practice of the political field, that is, finding a sociological perspective on the commentary which is offered to the public by media pundits whose interest lies in sustaining the exclusivity of the political game. The caveat here is that, for Bourdieu, this means doing sociology in a different way in order to avoid sociological analysis becoming the preserve of the defenders of the field of sociology. To counteract this danger, Bourdieu emphasised that sociological analysis needs to be the manifestation of the primary experience of practitioners. The way to resist reproduction is for individuals to activate their incorporated capital, the attitudes and values inherent in their social formation so as to subvert the ways in which moribund behaviour has become instituted. He suggested that we need Trojan horses, people who use their training to question its validity rather than to reproduce it. He cited Manet as such a revolutionary in art, and Courrèges in fashion, and this was also how he saw his own career.

These were Bourdieu's proposed solutions, but it may be too late for them. I leave it for you to reflect. Perhaps there is no longer a sphere of primary social experience to be resurrected. Media and social media may have usurped the power of primary, incorporated capital. In calling for its resurrection, was Bourdieu crying in the wilderness? Does he offer a hope for future resistance or should we recognize that he was a radical reactionary or, perhaps, a reactionary radical?

POSTSCRIPT

Towards a new quietism

The introduction stated that the book would present a sequence of objective textual presentations interspersed with accounts of the socio-intellectual contexts which generated them. It is clear now in retrospect that the posited dialectical relationship has not remained of the same kind over time, or that I have not presented it in the same way. I find it useful to clarify this by deploying the distinction Bourdieu made between three types of 'cultural capital'.[1] He distinguished between 'incorporated capital' which corresponds with the characteristics acquired in childhood, either by nature or by nurture, and 'objectivated capital' which is a kind of personal capital which is supported by adherence to cultures and values which are current in society at any time, whether modern or traditional. By attaching ourselves to these objective cultural values, whether, as Bourdieu analysed in *La Distinction*,[2] these involve commitment, for instance, to football or to classical music, we construct our social identities in ways which are partly conditioned by our inherited dispositions but may diverge from them significantly. These affiliations may be transient. We may choose to redefine ourselves by giving up going to football matches and by going instead (or as well) to concerts of classical music. Bourdieu's third type is 'instituted capital' by which he meant that some affiliations become permanent in such a way that our identities become fixed by association with them. Educational and professional qualifications and associated employment positions are examples.

Bourdieu developed this tripartite definition of cultural capital in 1979 when he was realising that his earlier broad conception of 'cultural capital' was inadequate. His earlier assumption was that our life-choices are softly predetermined by our inheritance. This was a 'traditional' or 'modernist' assumption. The specification of 'objectivated' capital was a recognition that, with the decline of the traditional family unit, we construct

---

1. Bourdieu (1979a). See my detailed discussion of this article in Robbins, 2019, 191–96.
2. Bourdieu (1979b, 1986).

our identities much more by reference to a constantly fluctuating market of attitudes and values. Bourdieu still wanted to ground the objectivated in the incorporated but this new recognition was an acknowledgement of the influence of 'postmodernism'. Having released his tight grip on the influence of inherited dispositions, Bourdieu, however, sought some stability in positing the third category which depends on the recognition of institutionalised values which, therefore, still regulate the fluidity of the postmodern market of values and identities. It remains, I think, an open question whether the distinction between 'objectivated' and 'instituted' is valid. Indeed, it may be that this differentiation occurred to Bourdieu at precisely the moment when he accepted the chair of sociology at the Collège de France and hence publicly affiliated himself with an institution possessing objective, historically established, credentials. In an article such as 'Le titre et le poste' (Bourdieu and Boltanski, 1975) he had shown that educational qualifications are pawns in a game of class differentiation and, as such, are malleable objectivities rather than indications of absolute achievement. Bourdieu always recognised that he was an 'oblate', someone who accepted that he had some disinclination to criticise an educational system which had provided him with the capacity to make that criticism, and this angst was apparent in the awkward way in which he presented himself for legitimation before the other professors at the Collège de France in his inaugural lecture.[3] In short, he was reflexively aware that his conceptualisations were functions of his personal trajectory as well as tools for explaining it.

I can point to a similar situation when I review my contextualisaton of the six passages contained in this book. The significant difference is that halfway through the trajectory that I have outlined I absorbed Bourdieu's conceptualisation into my self-understanding. The familial background described in Chapter 1 was lived unreflectingly. It was my primary experience. The fact that the context was apolitical was not a part of my consciousness. Application and admission to a grammar school was not my 'choice'. These were enactments of the aspirations of my parents. Their decision to encourage me to work towards entry to the school was an unconscious determination that I should become associated with the institutional distinction which it supplied. My father was a manual worker and, before she married, my mother was a clerical worker, both leaving school at the age of 14. The grammar school institution provided access to objectivated cultures which were not available to me at home. I imbibed scholarly cultures while I had very little exposure to contemporary cultures, such as, for instance, pop music. The curriculum was set, but I had no sense that it was a contingent reflection of the educational system

---

3. Bourdieu (1982; 1990, 177–98).

into which I had been inserted. My preferences within the curriculum were indicative of an elective affinity – part choice and part entrenched predisposition – whereby I reconciled my incorporated nonconformist convictions with consecrated texts in an objectivated humanities curriculum. I was involved in a process of existential self-definition through the study of history and texts rather than in a process by which I acquired knowledge, science or skill. I had begun with inherited attitudes and I acquired opinions through the amalgamation of incorporated and objectivated capitals. I formed some opinions which could be said to be political, such as hostility to nuclear warfare and to aristocratic privilege, but these were primarily moral. Chapter 1 is indicative of a dabbling with explanatory science in relation to a topic which was attractive because of the drama whereby a politician was trying to extricate himself from his privileged inheritance.

Admission to Cambridge prolonged the mutual reinforcement of objectivated and instituted capital which had been transmitted by my school. My studies continued to be the medium for an existential process. My topic for PhD research set up an objective exploration of a case study of the reconciliation of the discourses of science and literature in the context of redefinitions of the status of dogmatic Christian belief. There had been no real decision to undertake research. Examination success had made continuation seem to be the next logical step. Mixed with what might now seem self-indulgence was a kind of missionary motivation, a desire to transmit an understanding of an issue which seemed current in the contemporary 'two cultures' debate. This same motivation, perhaps, lay beneath the next irrational 'choice', which was to seek employment as a university teacher.

It was at this point that I lost much of the instituted capital which had accreted in the previous 20 years. Social change at the end of the 1960s meant that a complement of new staff had already been taken on by the 'new' universities and that there was no longer much opportunity for the kind of scholar that I appeared to be. I was fortunate to find a post to teach English literature in a new institution but, as such, it was an institution which possessed no instituted capital. The aura of a Cambridge graduate had ambiguous value in my early years at North East London Polytechnic. It was thought to be a disadvantage as far as the social mission of the institution was concerned, but it was of value in legitimating pedagogic innovation during the process of receiving accreditation from the CNAA. For 15 years, I forgot any previous aspiration to publish the findings of my research. Instead, I devoted myself to attempting to establish courses which would offer students less formally qualified than traditional university entrants the chance to be involved in an educational process which, in effect, replicated my previous experiences. Students were encouraged to define their incorporated identities on arrival and were given the opportunity to develop those identities by appropriating those aspects of the objectivated intellectual discourses on offer within the institution which were relevant to their personally projected self-objectivation. The courses by independent study obliged students to make explicit their choices of programmes of study, whether academic or vocational. Students were asked to make forward projections for their lives, to make explicit the kinds of 'choices' which I had made unreflexively in my career. The only research which I undertook in these years was designed to evaluate the process of independent study either directly by studying the trajectories of students or analogously by analysing comparable historical processes or situations. In harmony with the mission of the polytechnic, I regarded my pedagogic actions and my commentaries on them as political statements. I could see that good students were penalised as a consequence of the supposedly low status of the institution within the higher education system, and I endeavoured to combat this discrimination in my practice and in theoretical work. It was only towards the end of the life of the School for Independent Study that I met Pierre Bourdieu. At first his concepts provided me with a language in which to articulate my findings in educational research. After the closure of the School, I began to reconstruct the intellectual identity which had been put on hold in the previous 15 years. The short period as a Head of Department at the end of the 1990s was an opportunity to resurrect some unity between my thought and educational practice. Instead of simply using Bourdieu's concepts, I worked additionally to understand the sociopolitical and philosophical background to the emergence of those concepts. Just as Bourdieu commented that he wrote 'under the aegis'[4] of Pascal, deriving his own authority from the work of the seventeenth-century scientist and philosopher, securing capital by association, so I increasingly wrote under his aegis as well as about him. I acquired objectivated capital through my publications. I never acquired instituted capital through association with any body thought to possess pre-existing status, and retirement is now a deinstitutionalised condition.

Bourdieu's tripartite categorisation of cultural capital can be applied to understand our current sociopolitical situation in the United Kingdom. We all live in these three modes, but the balance between them has shifted significantly. In my lifetime, the importance of reference to social or familial background has noticeably declined. The teaching profession may deploy the Bourdieusian concepts of habitus and cultural capital in reflecting on classroom communications, but I suspect that students themselves, instead, do not consider their identities to have been preconditioned, even softly, by early parental influence. Identity construction is much more a question of managing

---

4. See Bourdieu (1997, 9; 2000, 1).

choice within a range of available objectivated capitals. These capitals are increasingly autonomous, unregulated by reference to provenance. Even 'identity' itself is in the process of becoming commodified, detached from any notion of indigenous authenticity. Identity is specified more in terms of reified classifications than reflexively in terms of origins. Similarly, the educational process has become de-existentialised. The system is geared to defining the parameters of what learning is to be acquired so as to safeguard equality of opportunity and to eliminate disadvantage, but this is inimical to encouraging self-development based on personal reflection. Social media contribute to the domination of ungrounded objectivated capital. Identity construction is occurring in media exchange just as the truthfulness of news is in dispute as offered in broadcasting and journalism. The referentiality of information is under threat. 'Populism' has become a constructed label which is divorced from the attitudes of people. The involvement of the public in politics has increased, but this participation is based more on the market exchange of opinions than on lived experience. When Bourdieu wrote 'Public Opinion Does Not Exist' in 1972 (in Bourdieu, 1980, 222–35; 1993b, 149–57) he argued that opinion polls constructed 'public opinion' by neglecting 'no responses' to surveys. That exclusion has now been superseded. Instead, we assimilate the discourse that pollsters and commentators offer us and believe that this constitutes political engagement.

If primary or inherited experience has been substantially discredited and replaced by surrogate inclusion in contrived discourse about self, society and others, there is perhaps a social struggle also between the claims of objectivated and instituted capitals. Instituted capital is predicated on privilege and historical precedents. The authority of 'the establishment' – the Church, the monarchy, the government, parliament, the judiciary – is increasingly held, almost as a rearguard action, to be above the commodity exchange of objectivated capital. The defence of the institution of marriage is another example. Politicians are not immune to this tension between capitals. As Bourdieu pointed out in the article discussed in Chapter 6B, the essence of politics is that in democratic society the field of political action and discourse should not be static but should be constantly open to modification to respond to changing circumstances. The structure is the message. Contemporary politicians need to retain reflexivity about their own primary experiences and offer their selves for election to parliament. Mass democracy requires that politicians should be sample citizens in parliament, designated installations rather than 'representatives'. The tendency, however, is for politicians to seek to establish a discrete professionalism as 'parliamentarians', dedicated to maintaining the autonomy of instituted practices, or, alternatively, to devote themselves to missions or causes abstracted in an objectivated market from the common concerns of their constituents. Just as David represented himself within the scene of Napoleon's enthronement,[5] so politicians need to retain a detached awareness of the artificial spectacle in which they are participating. As the discussion of Burke in Chapter 5B showed, Burke believed that he was in possession of knowledge of national traditions and needs which entitled him to reject the notion that he might reproduce, as a delegate, the views of the minority of the population of his constituency which constituted his electorate. A complexly diverse mass society requires neither political delegation nor a revival of post-aristocratic and post-bourgeois parliamentary privilege but a common recognition that members of parliament are individuals who appropriate instituted capital only temporarily, recognise that their authority is socially constructed, and acknowledge the constraints on their incorporated dispositions exacted both by the market of ideas and the traditions which accrue to the situation in which they work.

None of us is immune to this tension between cultural capitals. Like David, Bourdieu located himself within the model of social reality which he presented graphically in his *Homo Academicus* (Bourdieu, 1984, 1988). Sociological analysis is not transcendent but is immanently present in the models which it constructs. This meant that, for Bourdieu, sociological analyses are functions of the social positions of the analysts. By recommending that all persons should situate themselves socio-analytically in encounter with others, deploying in the process whatever kinds of capital they might bring to the exchange, Bourdieu was arguing for a social ontology.[6] Following the position adopted by Leibniz in his *Monadology* (1714), we are all 'entelechies' which interact in apparently random ways but, in fact, in accordance with an unknown pre-ordained purpose. Voltaire thought that the corollary of this view was a laissez-faire attitude which assumed that, all evidence to the contrary, we live in 'the best of possible worlds' (in *Candide*, 1759). Bourdieu's hostility to 'symbolic violence', the imposition of views on others by force, would seem to suggest a similar complacency in the face of necessity, but, as Steve Fuller has shown (in Grenfell, 2008, 171–81), Bourdieu operated in a philosophical tradition which recognises 'conatus', the inevitability of striving for change while acknowledging that other forces are in play, competing for domination. This is not laissez-faire, but, rather, a form of quietism.[7]

---

5. See the cover image.
6. Importantly, Bourdieu was committed to making a social ontology the field within which he practised, intellectually and socially. Unlike John Searle (Searle, 1995, 2010), for instance, he was not interested in establishing 'social ontology' as a philosophical position.
7. As will be clear from the discussion of Fénelon which follows, I am talking about 'quietism' as a social and moral position, and not as a philosophical stance. In

Fénelon's Mentor: A provocative illustration

François Fénelon (1651–1715) was appointed tutor to the Duke of Burgundy, grandson of Louis XIV, in 1689, and, a year later, tutor to the Duke of Anjou, the younger brother of the Duke of Burgundy. Fénelon was vigorously opposed by Bossuet (1627–1704) who had been tutor to Louis XIV's eldest child, the Dauphin, from 1670 to 1681. The Dauphin died in 1711. The Duke of Burgundy died in 1712. Neither Fénelon nor Bossuet had been tutor to the second son of the Duke of Burgundy who became Louis XV on the death of his great-grandfather in 1715, but the Duke of Anjou subsequently became Philip V of Spain. Although they had limited direct influence over the future monarch who reigned almost to the eve of the French Revolution, they both published treatises in which they outlined their principles. Both were Catholic archbishops, but Bossuet was an implacable opponent of Protestantism, significantly involved in the revocation in 1685 of the Edict of Nantes which, a century earlier, had recognised the rights of protestants, while Fénelon was attracted by the quietist views of Mme Guyon[8] who was influential at court because of the support initially given to her by Mme de Maintenon. Bossuet made a connection between the views of the Quietists and those of the Quakers in England. Bossuet was court preacher to Louis XIV and a forthright advocate of political absolutism and the divine right of kings, while Fénelon emphasised that monarchs exercise their authority only with the consent of their citizens. Fénelon probably began writing *Les Aventures de Télémaque* (The Adventures of Telemachus) in 1692, but the first full edition was not published until April 1699. In January 1697, Fénelon published his *Explication des maximes des saints sur la vie intérieure* (Explanation of the Sayings of the Saints about the Inner Life) which attempted to defend a spiritual inner life without admitting sympathy with Mme Guyon, but there followed a brutal exchange with Bossuet who attacked both Fénelon and Mme Guyon in his *Relation sur le quiétisme* (Commentary on Quietism) of 1698. Bossuet prevailed. In 1699, Fénelon was expelled from court to his archdiocese of Cambrai and deprived of his title and pension as royal tutor.

'Naturalism and Quietism', for instance, Rorty differentiates his own position from that of Wittgenstein which he regards as quietist (Rorty, 2007, 147–59), and Pettit makes the same differentiation in his 'Existentialism, Quietism, and Philosophy' (in Leiter, 2004, 300–327). Both are concerned to specify a function for academic philosophy more than to consider a social attitude.

8. Mme Guyon (1648–1717).

Les Aventures uses a framework derived from classical sources to give an account of the adventures of Telemachus as he tried to find his father, Ulysses, lost since Troy. Telemachus is accompanied by Mentor who advises him throughout and ensures that he gains wisdom from his experiences, learning from observation how monarchs should conduct themselves in relation to their people. In Book II, for instance, Telemachus recounts how Mentor recommended to him the way Sesostris ruled Egypt. Mentor drew his attention to the joy and abundance apparent in Egypt's 22,000 towns:

> He admired the good police in these towns, the justice exercised in favour of the poor against the rich, the good education of children – that they became accustomed to obedience, work, sobriety, the love of art and literature, exactness in respect of all religious ceremonies, *disinterestedness*, the desire for honour, fidelity towards men and fear of the gods, all of which every father inspired in his children. He never tired of admiring this beautiful orderliness. (Fénelon, 1995, 47, italics added)[9]

In Book V, Telemachus tells how Mentor commended the prosperity of Crete where they had landed:

> The more men there are in a country, the more they enjoy abundance provided they are laborious. They never have any need to be jealous of each other. The earth, that good mother, multiplies its gifts according to the number of its children who merit its fruits through their work. (Fénelon, 1995, 96).

Mentor praises the laws established by King Minos. Telemachus asks in what the king's authority consisted. Mentor replies:

> He has complete authority over the people, but the laws have complete authority over him. He has an absolute power to do good, and hands tied if he wants to do evil. The people entrust the laws to him as the most precious of all deposits, on condition that he will be the father of his subjects. They want a sole man to provide, by his wisdom and moderation, for the happiness of many men: and not that many men should, by their wretchedness and base servility, flatter the pride and indolence of a sole man. The king should have nothing above others, except what is needed either to support him in his difficult tasks or to

---

9. These are my translations. An English translation by Smollett was published in 1776.

impress on people respect for the person who has to uphold the laws. (Fénelon, 1995, 97)

In Book VII, Telemachus asks a Phoenician, Aboam, to describe the country of Betic[10] which he had visited. Aboam says:

> Every family is governed by its chief who, in effect, is its king. [...] All goods are common. The fruit from the trees, the vegetables from the earth, the milk from the herds, are so abundant riches that the people who are so sober and moderate have no need to distribute them. (Fénelon, 1995, 156)

Time after time, Mentor draws the attention of Telemachus to the harmony with the natural world and between people achieved as a direct consequence of the disposition of those in authority. Having fought alongside Idomineo in a just war (pretext for Mentor's presentation of his views on this concept), Telemachus returns to Salento[11] and asks Mentor to explain the transformations which he had effected in that society during his absence. Telemachus observed that there were no more magnificent buildings nor obvious affluence, but that he had everywhere seen 'honourable husbandry and prepared fields'. Which is worth more, Mentor asks,

> Either a splendid town, in marble, gold, and silver, with a neglected and sterile countryside, or a cultivated and fertile countryside, with a mediocre town, modest in its customs. (Fénelon, 1995, 367)

Telemachus learns the key to this social harmony when he decides to search for his father in the Underworld. In Book XIV he speaks to dead kings – those condemned to suffering for having abused their power, and then to all the dead kings who had previously governed men wisely. He found that these were bathed in light, an illumination which suffused their beings. In death, these kings see, feel and breathe this spiritual light,

> it generates in them an inexhaustible source of peace and joy. They are plunged into this abyss of joy, like fish in the sea. They have no more wish for anything. They have everything, without having anything, for this taste of light quenches the thirst of their heart, all their desires are

---

10. A region which corresponds roughly with current Andalusia.
11. A town which Idomineo had established in Apulia, Italy.

sated and their completeness lifts them above everything which empty
and starving men search for on earth. (Fénelon, 1995, 317–18)

This is the mystical language of Mme Guyon. The pure light is the 'pure love'
which, according to Quietism, should govern all our actions. We are right into
the 'amour pur' controversy between Fénelon and Bossuet which took place
in the last few years of the seventeenth century and in which Leibniz became
involved.[12] In his *Explication des maximes des saints*, Fénelon distinguished between
five categories of love, the last of which was 'pure love'. This was characterised
by disinterestedness or indifference. He wrote that 'every interested love [...]
is a love unworthy of Him [God]' (Fénelon, 1697, 20) and also that 'as indifference is love itself, it is a very real and positive principle – it is not at all a
stupid indolence' (Fénelon, 1697, 51). Stripped of its association with the mystical spirituality of Mme de Guyon, the essence of Fénelon's position was that
it is perfectly possible to suppose that monarchs and people can operate out
of motives which are not dictated by self-interest and that this capacity is the
basis of a harmonious society. As one commentator on the pure love debate
has stated, Fénelon's book was 'the first systematic attempt to elaborate the a
priori schemes of radical disinterestedness' (Terestchenko, 2008). We should
not be confused by the ambivalent nuances of terminology. Indifference is 'the
making of no difference between conflicting parties' (*Oxford English Dictionary*).
It is irenical. It cultivates impartiality. It shares a similar ambivalence with
'indiscriminate'. It is not lazy or random. In acknowledging what Lyotard
called the 'différend' (Lyotard, 1983, 1988), it recognises difference without
allowing it significance. It accepts diversity without permitting discrimination.
It encourages unconditioned alterity.

Fénelon's vision of harmonious societies had elements of pre-lapsarian,
pastoral fantasy. His vision for social and political harmony was dependent
on a system managed by an enlightened ruler, someone who held that position by moral example and thereby secured a matching moral response in
the population. In England, Fénelon's contemporary John Locke (1632–1704)
was outlining the conditions which would allow a population to challenge the
authority of its monarch. In his *Two Treatises on Government* (1690) he distinguished between two sectors of the population – those exercising 'express' and
those exercising 'tacit' consent to the authority of the monarch. The former
had the capacity, through parliament, to use reason to oppose the abuse of
power, whereas the latter were unreasoning bystanders. Unlike Locke, Fénelon
showed little interest in the deployment of reason to restrict the authority of

---

12. In 1697, Leibniz responded in a letter to a request from the Electress Sophie of
    Hanover (mother of George I of England) for his views on the question.

the monarch through legal checks and balances. Social order should be consolidated pre-rationally in a state of ontological harmony.

I have recently translated and introduced a text produced at the end of World War II by the équipe d'Uriage entitled *Vers le style du XXe siècle*.[13] The main conviction which united a disparate group of authors was that the parliamentary government which had characterised the Third Republic had become moribund. Several of the authors were particularly influenced by the work of Emmanuel Mounier (1905–1950) who, in turn, was influenced by Charles Péguy (1873–1914). Péguy had been a supporter of Jean Jaurès (1859–1914) but he turned against his socialism. In *Notre Jeunesse*, he famously coined the slogan that 'tout commence en mystique et finit en politique' (everything begins in mystique and ends in politics) (Péguy, 1993, 115) citing as evidence the way in which the campaign in support of Dreyfus against anti-semitism had started as an apolitical moral campaign but had ended in being appropriated by the political agenda of socialism. The 'personalists' associated with Mounier believed that society could be reconstructed after World War II by initiating a programme of moral and civil education which would be transformative by bypassing political and religious institutions. They wanted to establish an 'order' within society which would be dedicated to its moral rejuvenation.

The movement of thought that I have traced in this book has led to a similar scepticism about the current capacity of politics to improve our lives. This could be seen as a revival of a dormant nonconformity, an inclination to celebrate a greater degree of separateness from political struggle than the current alliance between politics and media seems to permit. The solution, however, is not to reject politics but, instead, to bring political behaviour into an accord with contemporary social behaviour. This involves dismissing the representative model which is the legacy of Locke's argument that government can be constitutionally controlled by a rational minority acting on behalf of an irrational majority. Control should not be based on a putative rationality which is itself culturally distinct but on ontological indifference.

In 1989, Bourdieu published 'Un acte désintéressé est-il possible? (Is a disinterested act possible?). He commented that

> Primary a-politicism, which continues to grow because the political field tends increasingly to close in on itself and to function without reference to its clientele (a bit like the artistic field in other words), rests on a sort of confused consciousness of this deep complicity between adversaries inserted within the same field: they fight with each other, but they are at

---

13. Robbins (2021).

least in agreement on the object of their disagreement. (Bourdieu, 1994, 152–53, my translation)

We cannot allow politics to continue to be a self-fulfilling process of 'representation' played out before a population whose docility can no longer be assumed. We should reject the notion of absolute asocial individuality and also reject the similarly metaphysical notion of the transcendent sovereign state.[14] We should regenerate the idea that all forms of participation in society are mutually recognised public service duties rather than expressions of individual rights. This might restore the possibility that politicians might be encouraged to perform, functionally and provisionally, just as first among equals.

---

14. I am recommending the public law theory of Léon Duguit (1859–1928).

REFERENCES

Alpert, H., 1937, 'France's First University Course in Sociology', *American Sociological Review*, 2, 3: 311–17.

Althusser, L., and E. Balibar, 1970, *Reading Capital*, London, New Left Books.

Aron, R., 1981, *La sociologie allemande contemporaine*, Paris : Presses Universitaires de France.

Arnold, M., 1963 [1869], *Culture & Anarchy*, ed. J. Dover Wilson, Cambridge, Cambridge University Press.

Arzt, H. -G., ed., 1994, *Europaïsche Qualifikation durch deutsch-französische Ausbildung? Die Bedeutung der Unterschiede nationaler Bildungssysteme für die internationale wirtschaftliche Zusammenarbeit*, Neue Ludwigsburger Beitrage, Bd. 4., Deutsch-Französisches Institut, Ludwigsburg.*

Benney, M., and P. Geiss, 1950, 'Social Class and Politics in Greenwich', *British Journal of Sociology*, 1, 4: 310–27.

Bianchi, L., J. Ferrari and A. Postigliola, eds, 2009, *Kant et les Lumières européennes/Kant e l'Illuminismo europeo*, Naples: Editions Liguori; Paris: Librairie Philosophique Vrin.

Birch, A. H., and P. Campbell, 1950, 'Voting Behaviour in a Lancashire Constituency', *British Journal of Sociology*, 1, 3: 197–208.

Bourdieu, P., 1971, 'L'opinion publique n'existe pas', *Noroit*, 155.

——, 1972, *Esquisse d'une théorie de la pratique*, Geneva: Droz.

——, 1975, 'L'ontologie politique de Martin Heidegger', *Actes de la recherche en sciences sociales*, 5–6: 109–56.

——, 1977, *Outline of a Theory of Practice*, Cambridge: Cambridge University Press.

——, 1979a, 'Les trois états du capital culturel', *Actes de la recherche en sciences sociales*, 30: 3–6.

——, 1979b, *La distinction. Critique sociale du jugement*, Paris: Éd. de Minuit.

——, 1980, *Questions de sociologie*, Paris: Éd. de Minuit.

——, 1982a, 'Goffman, le découvreur de l'infiniment petit', *Le Monde*, 4 December 1982: 1 and 30.

——, 1982b, *Leçon sur la leçon*, Paris: Éd. de Minuit.

——, 1984, *Homo Academicus*, Paris: Éd. de Minuit.

——, 1986, *Distinction. A Social Critique of the Judgement of Taste*, London: Routledge & Kegan Paul.

——, 1988, *Homo Academicus*, Cambridge, Polity.

——, 1990, *In Other Words. Essays towards a Reflexive Sociology*, Cambridge: Polity.

——, 1993a, 'L'Impromptu de Bruxelles', *Cahiers de l'École des sciences philosophiques et religieuses*, 14: 33–48.

——, 1993b, *Sociology in Question*, London: Sage.

——, 1994, *Raisons pratiques*, Paris: Seuil.

——, 1997, *Méditations pascaliennes*, Paris: Seuil.

————, 2000, *Pascalian Meditations*, Cambridge: Polity.

————, 2002a, *Interventions1961–2001: Science sociale et action politique*, ed. F. Poupeau and T. Discepolo, Marseille: Agone.

————, 2002b, *Le bal des célibataires. Crise de la société en Béarn*, Paris: Éd du Seuil.

————, 2004, *Esquisse pour une auto-analyse*, Paris: Raisons d'Agir.

————, 2007, *Sketch for a Self-Analysis*, Oxford: Polity.

————, 2008, *The Bachelors Ball. The Crisis of Peasant Society in Béarn*, Cambridge: Polity.

Bourdieu, P., and L. Boltanski, 1975, 'Le titre et le poste. Rapports entre le système de production et le système de reproduction', *Actes de la recherche en sciences sociales*, 2: 95–107.

————, 1976, 'La production de l'idéologie dominante', *Actes de la recherche en sciences sociales*, 2–3: 3–73.

Bourdieu, P., and J. -C. Passeron, 1970, *La reproduction. Éléments pour une théorie du système d'enseignement*, Paris: Éd de Minuit.

————, 1977, *Reproduction in Education, Society and Culture*, London: Sage.

Bourdieu, P., and L. Wacquant, 1998, 'Sur les ruses de la raison impérialiste', *Actes de la recherche en sciences sociales*, 121–22: 109–18.

————,1999, 'On the Cunning of Imperialist Reason', trans. D. Robbins and L. Wacquant, *Theory, Culture and Society*, 16, 1: 41–58.

Bourdieu, P., J. -C. Chamboredon and J. -C. Passeron, 1968, *Le métier de sociologue*, Paris: Mouton-Bordas.

————, 1991, *The Craft of Sociology*, New York: de Gruyter.

Brubaker, R., 1992, *Citizenship and Nationhood in France and Germany*, Cambridge, MA: Harvard University Press.

Butler, D. E., 1952, *The British General Election of 1951*, London: Macmillan.

————, 1953, *The Electoral System in Britain 1918–1951*, Oxford: Oxford University Press.

————, 1955, *The British General Election of 1955*, London: Macmillan.

————, 1958, *The Study of Political Behaviour*, London: Hutchinson University Library.

Butler, D. E., and R. Rose, 1959, *The British General Election of 1959*, London: Macmillan.

Carlyle, T., 1845, *Oliver Cromwell's Letters and Speeches, With Elucidation*, 4 volumes. London: Chapman and Hall.

Clark, T. N., 1973, *Prophets and Patrons: The French University and the Emergence of the Social Sciences*, Cambridge, MA: Harvard University Press.

Cohen, P., ed., 1999, *New Ethnicities, Old Racisms?*, London: Zed Books.

Durkheim, E., 1964 [1933], *The Division of Labor in Society*, trans. G. Simpson, New York, The Free Press.

————, 1997, *Montesquieu. Quid Secundatus Politicae Scientiae Instituendae Contulerit*, ed. W. Watts Miller, Oxford: Durkheim Press.

————, 2002 [1924], *Sociologie et philosophie*, préface by C. Bouglé (1924), in B. Karsenti, ed. (2002), Paris, PUF.

Endo, K., 1999, *The Presidency of the European Commission under Jacques Delors: The Politics of Shared Leadership*, Houndmills, Basingstoke: Macmillan/St. Martin's.

Eribon, D., 1992, *Michel Foucault*, London, Faber & Faber.

Fénelon, F., 1697, *Explication des maximes des saints*, Paris. https://gallica.bnf.fr/ark:/12148/btv1b8608261d/f6.item.

Fénelon, F., 1995, *Les Aventures de Télémaque*, ed. J. Le Brun, Paris: Gallimard.

Ferrari, J., Ruffing, M., Theis, R., and Vollet, M., eds, 2005, *Kant et la France – Kant und Frankreich*, Hildesheim, Zurich: Olms.

Foucault, M., 2008, *Introduction to Kant's Anthropology*, ed. and trans. R. Nigro and K. Briggs, Los Angeles: Semiotext(e).

Fowler, B., ed., 2000. *Reading Bourdieu on Society and Culture*, Oxford: Blackwell.

Goffman, E., 1969, 1959, *The Presentation of Self in Everyday Life*, London: Penguin.

———, 1961, *Asylums*, London: Penguin.

———, 1971, *Relations in Public*, London: Penguin.

Grant, C., 1994, *Delors: Inside the House That Jacques Built*, London; Nicholas Brealey.

Grenfell, M., ed., 2008, *Pierre Bourdieu. Key Concepts*, Stocksfield: Acumen.

———, ed., 2012, *Pierre Bourdieu. Key Concepts*, 2nd ed., Stocksfield: Acumen.

Grenfell, M., and M. Kelly, eds, 1999, *Pierre Bourdieu: Language, Culture and Education. Theory into Practice*. Berne: Peter Lang.

Habermas, 1989 [1962], *The Structural Transformation of the Public Sphere*, Cambridge: Polity.

Hall, D. D., 2019, *The Puritans. A Transatlantic History*, Princeton, NJ: Princeton University Press.

Halsey, A. H., 2004, *A History of Sociology in Britain. Science, Literature, and Society*, Oxford: Oxford University Press.

Jackson, B., and D. Marsden, 1962, *Education and the Working Class*, London: Routledge.

Jay, B., 1994, 'History Teaching at the Universities of Liverpool and Sussex, 1958–1968', GRASP, Working Paper 9, University of East London.*

Kedward, R., 2005, *La Vie en bleu. France and the French since 1900*, London: Penguin Books.

Lazarsfeld, P., B. Berelson and H. Gaudet, 1948, *The People's Choice*, New York: Columbia University Press.

Leiter, B., ed., 2004, *The Future for Philosophy*, Oxford: Oxford University Press.

Lyotard, J. -F., 1954, *La phénoménologie*, Paris: PUF.

———, 1979, *La condition postmoderne*, Paris: Minuit.

———, 1983, *Le différend*, Paris: Minuit.

———, 1986a, *The Postmodern Condition*, Manchester: Manchester University Press.

———, 1986b, *L'enthousiasme. La critique kantienne de l'histoire*, Paris: Galilée.

———, 1988, *The Differend. Phrases in Dispute*, Minneapolis: University of Minnesota Press.

———, 1991, *Leçons sur l'analytique du sublime*, Paris: Galilée.

———, 1994, *Lessons on the Analytic of the Sublime*, Stanford, CA: Stanford University Press.

McCallum, R. B., 1954, 'The Study of Psephology', *Parliamentary Affairs*, VIII, 4: 508–13.

McCallum, R. B., and A. Readman, 1947, *The British General Election of 1945*, London: Oxford University Press.

Merleau-Ponty, M., 1945, *Phénoménologie de la perception*, Paris: Gallimard.

———, 1960, *Signes*, Paris: Gallimard.

———, 1962, *Phenomenology of Perception*, London: Routledge & Kegan Paul.

———, 1964, *Signs*, Evanston, IL: Northwestern University Press.

Milne, R. S., and H. C. Mackenzie, 1954, *Straight Fight. A Study of Voting Behaviour in the Constituency of Bristol North-East at the General Election of 1951*, London: Hansard Society.

———, 1958, *Marginal Seat, 1955: A Study of Voting Behaviour in the Constituency of Bristol North-East at the General Election of 1955*, London: Hansard Society.

Otaka, T., 2022 [1932], *Outline of a Theory of Social Association*, ed. D. Robbins, Peter Lang.

Passeron, J. C., 2013 [1991], *Sociological Reasoning*, ed. D. Robbins, Oxford, Bardwell Press.

Passeron, J. C., and Grignon, C., 1989, *Le savant et le populaire*, Paris, Seuil.

Péguy, C., 1993, *Notre Jeunesse, précédé par De la raison*, ed. J. Bastaire, Paris: Gallimard.

Ringer, F., 1969, *The Decline of the German Mandarins. The German Academic Community, 1890–1933*, Cambridge, MA: Harvard University Press.

Ringer, F., 1992, *Fields of Knowledge: French Academic Culture in Comparative Perspective, 1890–1920*, Cambridge: Cambridge University Press and Maison des Sciences de l'Homme.

Robbins, D., ed., 1978a, *Britain and the EEC: Admission to Higher Education*, NELP, International Office.

————, 1978b, 'The Promotion of Part-Course Transfer in Europe', in D. Robbins, ed., *Britain and the EEC: Admission to Higher Education*, NELP, International Office.

————, 1981, 'Occasional Papers in Course Development, *1973-1978*', School for Independent Study, UEL, Research paper 5.*

————, 1982, 'Educational and Occupational Mobility in Europe: Opportunities for Study and Work', NELP, International Office. Report prepared for the Commission of the European Communities.

————, 1988, *The Rise of Independent Study. The Politics and the Philosophy of an Educational Innovation, 1970-1987*, Milton Keynes: Open University Press, co-published with the SRHE.

————, 1991, *The Work of Pierre Bourdieu*, Milton Keynes: Open University Press.

————, 1992, 'Business and Management Education in England since 1965', in *Les Institutions de Formation des Cadres Dirigeants. Etude Comparée*, Maison des Sciences de l'Homme, Paris.*

————, 1994a, Preface to *History Teaching at the Universities of Liverpool and Sussex, 1958-1968* by B. Jay, GRASP, Working Paper 9, University of East London.

————, 1994b, 'The Particular Universities of Europe', *European Update*, UEL, No 13: 19–20.*

————, 1994c, 'Transnational Learning in the Field of History', in H-G. Arzt, ed., *Europaische Qualifikation durch deutsch-franzosische Ausbildung? Die Bedeutung der Unterschiede nationaler Bildungssysteme für die internationale wirtschaftliche Zusammenarbeit*, Neue Ludwigsburger Beitrage, Bd. 4, Deutsch-Franzosisches Institut, Ludwigsburg

————, 1995a, Review of *Histoire des universités* by C. Charle and J. Verger, *Actes de la recherche en sciences sociales*, no. 106–7: 126–27.

————, 1995b, 'Business Studies. The Market of Institutions and the Labour Market. An English Case-Study', in D. Broady, M. de Saint Martin and M. Palme, eds, *Les Elites. Formation, Reconversion, Internationalisation*, Centre de sociologie de l'éducation et de la culture, EHESS, Paris, & Forskningsgruppen för utbildnings- och kultursociologi, Lararhogskolan, Stockholm.*

————, 1996a, 'The University of East London and the Université de Paris VIII – an Elective Affinity?' *European Update*, UEL. No. 15: 17–20.*

————, 1996b, 'Different Ways of Thinking about Society in Europe', UEL, Department of Combined Social Sciences, Politics Area Working Paper.*

————, 1997, 'SOCRATES: Inter-University or Inter-Faculty Links?', in *European Update*, UEL, No. 16: 16–18.*

————, 1999, 'Bourdieu on Language and Education: Conjunction or Parallel Development', in M. Grenfell and M. Kelly, eds, *Pierre Bourdieu: Language, Culture and Education. Theory into Practice*, Berne: Peter Lang.

————, 2000a, 'The English Intellectual Field in the 1790s and the Creative Project of Samuel Taylor Coleridge – an Application of Bourdieu's Cultural Analysis', in B. Fowler, ed., *Reading Bourdieu on Society and Culture*, Oxford: Blackwell, 186–98.

————, 2000b, *Bourdieu and Culture*, London: Sage.

————, ed., 2000c, *Pierre Bourdieu*, 4 vols, London: Sage.

————, 2001, 'Lévy-Bruhl on Leibniz. A Translation of an Extract from L. Lévy-Bruhl: *Allemagne depuis Leibniz* (1890), with a Critical Introduction', Social Politics Working Papers, 15.*

————, 2003, 'Durkheim through the Eyes of Bourdieu', *Durkheim Studies/Etudes Durkheimiennes*, 9: 23–39.

————, ed., 2004, *Jean-François Lyotard*, 3 vols, London: Sage; New Delhi: Thousand Oaks.

————, 2005, 'Kant, Cassirer et Bourdieu', in J. Ferrari, M. Ruffing, R. Theis and M. Vollet, eds, *Kant et la France – Kant und Frankreich*, Hildesheim, Zurich: Olms .

————, 2006a, *On Bourdieu, Education and Society*, Oxford: Bardwell Press.

————, 2006b, 'A Social Critique of Judgement', *Theory, Culture and Society*, 23, 6: 1–24.

————, 2008, 'Theory of Practice', in M. Grenfell, ed., *Pierre Bourdieu. Key Concepts*, Stocksfield: Acumen, 27–40.

————, 2009a, 'Kant et les lumières anglaises', in L. Bianchi, J. Ferrari and A. Postigliola, eds, *Kant et les Lumières européennes / Kant e l'Illuminismo europeo*, , Naples: Editions LiguorI, 157–64.

————, 2009b, 'Publication: A Theoretical Preamble'. Editor's introduction to *Crossing Conceptual Boundaries*, 1: 4–27, School of Humanities and Social Sciences, University of East London.

————, 2010, 'Cambridge in the 1960s: Intellectual Debate as a Form of Institutional *méconnaissance*', *Cambridge Anthropology*, 29, 2: 73–90.

————, 2011a, *French Post War Social Theory: International Knowledge Transfer*, London: Sage.

————, 2011b, 'John Stuart Mill and Auguste Comte: A Trans-cultural Comparative Epistemology of the Social Sciences', *Journal of Classical Sociology*, 11, 1: 1–24.

————, 2011c, 'Sociological Analysis and Socio-Political Change: Juxtaposing Elements of the Work of Bourdieu, Passeron and Lyotard', in M. Benson and R. Munro, eds, *Sociological Routes and Political Roots*, Oxford: Wiley-Blackwell / *Sociological Review*, 117–34.

————, 2012, 'Theory of Practice', in M. Grenfell, ed., *Pierre Bourdieu. Key Concepts*, 2nd ed., Stocksfield: Acumen, 26–40.

————, 2014, *Cultural Relativism and International Politics*, Los Angeles: Sage.

————, ed., 2016, *The Anthem Companion to Bourdieu*, London: Anthem Press.

————, 2019, *The Bourdieu Paradigm. The Origins and Evolution of an Intellectual Social Project*, Manchester: Manchester University Press.

————, 2020, 'Independent Study', in Rustin and Poynter, eds, *Building a Radical University. A History of the University of East London*, London: Lawrence Wishart, 207–24.

————, 2021, *Towards a New Humanity: The Uriage Manifesto, 1945*, Oxford / Vienna: Peter Lang.

Robbins, D., B. Adams and J. Stephens, 1981, 'Validity and Validation in Higher Education'. Research report and four research papers (Research Papers 1–4), NELP, SIS.

Robinson, E., 1968, *The New Polytechnics. The People's Universities*, Harmondsworth: Penguin.

Rorty, R., 2007, *Philosophy as Cultural Politics*, Philosophical Papers, Volume 4, Cambridge: Cambridge University Press.

Rosanvallon, P., 2004, *Le modèle politique français. La société civile contre le jacobinisme*, Paris: Editions du Seuil.

Rustin, M., and G. Poynter, eds, 2020, *Building a Radical University. A History of the University of East London*, London: Lawrence Wishart.

Schutz, A., 1967 [1932]. *The Phenomenology of the Social World*, Evanston, IL: Northwestern University.

Searle, J. R., 1995, *The Construction of Social Reality*, London: Penguin.

————, 2010, *Making the Social World. The Structure of Human Civilization*, Oxford: Oxford University Press.

Terestchenko, M., 2008, 'The Dispute on Genuine Love in the 17th Century between Fénelon and Bossuet', *Revue du MAUSS*, 32, 2: 173–84.

Thatcher, J., N. Ingram, C. Burke and J. Abrahams, 2016, *Bourdieu: The Next Generation*, London: Routledge.

Young, M. F. D., ed., 1971, *Knowledge and Control: New Directions for the Sociology of Education*, London: Collier-Macmillan.

Zeldin, T., 1980, *France 1848-1945. Intellect and Pride*, Oxford: Oxford University Press.

INDEX